EASY STORIES IN ENGLISH FOR ADVANCED LEARNERS

10 FAIRY TALES TO TAKE YOUR ENGLISH FROM OK TO GOOD AND FROM GOOD TO GREAT

ARIEL GOODBODY

This is a work of fiction. Names, characters, places, and incidents either are the product of the author's imagination or are used fictitiously. Any resemblance to actual persons, living or dead, events, or locales is entirely coincidental.

Copyright © 2021 by Ariel Goodbody

All rights reserved. No part of this book may be reproduced in any form on by an electronic or mechanical means, including information storage and retrieval systems, without permission in writing from the publisher, except by a reviewer who may quote brief passages in a review.

Cover design by Geoffrey Bunting

Print ISBN 978-1-914968-03-7

Some of these stories were originally released at EasyStoriesInEnglish.com

CONTENTS

Why You Must Read	v
The North Wind and the Sun	1
Strange Friends	5
The Very Hungry Dragon	11
Doggo and Kitty Do Their Laundry	18
Doggo and Kitty Tear Their Trousers	27
Doggo and Kitty Bake a Cake	35
Sleeping Beauty	44
One-Eyed, Two-Eyed, Three-Eyed	55
The Boy Who Knew No Fear	72
Cinderella	93
Author's Note	117
Vocabulary Explanations and References	121
Image Attributions	143

WHY YOU MUST READ

'Why do I need to read in English?'

I get this question a lot from students. They argue that, as long as they're going to classes, doing their homework and watching films in English, there's no need to sit down with something as boring and old-fashioned as a book.

Well, to put it bluntly[1], they're wrong. In fact, reading is the best thing you can do to learn English, and I'm here to tell you why.

Firstly, reading skills are more important than ever, whether that be in English or your native language. In 2006, only 1 in 100 people went to university. Now, it's 7 in 100[2]. All jobs, from office workers to mechanics, require far more reading and writing than a century ago[3]. The competition is higher, and readers win.

Secondly, reading is the best way to improve proficiency[4] in English *overall*. Yes, you heard me right. Reading will improve your speaking, writing, vocabulary and grammar far more efficiently than any other method. It won't improve your listening skills, but it will give you the vocabulary necessary to train your ear[5] quickly.

But it's not just any reading we're talking about. In school, you probably read lots in English. Boring textbooks and dry[6] stories with exercises at the end.

No, we're not talking about that. We're talking about reading for *pleasure*.

That means reading a book you enjoy because you enjoy it. Not because your teacher told you to. Not because it's what you're 'supposed' to read to improve your English. No questions, no book reports. Just pure, unfiltered[7] pleasure.

'Yeah, right!' you're probably thinking. 'That's too good to be true.'

Let me show you.

In 1965, an experiment was carried out in juvenile delinquent reform centres[8] in America[9]. One group of the students were given free books. They made sure they were exciting books that would appeal to young boys, such as *James Bond*. But unlike most reading programmes, they were not required to read the books. They were simply given them. They could throw the books away, give them back, or draw on the pages, and nobody would punish them for it.

But the boys *did* read them. They read a lot of them. Some of them read a book every two days.

At the end of two years, they tested the students. Not only did their reading and writing greatly improve, so did their attitude towards school. But the students who were not on this programme stayed the same. In fact, some of them got *worse* over the two years.

This isn't just for native speakers, either. A study of English as a Second Language (ESL) students in the Fiji islands[10] looked at three methods: traditional English teaching, sustained silent reading[11], and a more conventional reading programme, where the teachers read aloud to the students[12].

By the end of the first year, students taught with the two reading methods had a 15 month advantage in English ability, compared to the 6.5 months of the traditional method. When the study was replicated[13] in Singapore, the students who did only sustained silent reading did better on grammar tests than the students who had taken *only* grammar classes!

When we do grammar exercises, we try to memorise[14] the rules of the language. When we read, we *absorb* them.

But I know what you're thinking: 'That's all well and good, but when I pick up a book in English, it's too hard for me! I get bored of looking up words, and I give up after a few minutes.'

That's why I wrote this book. It is designed to make you fall in love with reading, by providing fun, familiar stories that are easy to understand.

The stories gradually increase in difficulty and length, so that you can feel a sense of progression and success at the end. Most of them were originally released on my podcast[15], *Easy Stories in English*, but they have been rewritten and improved for this book, as well as having a version for each language level. They are a mix of classic and less popular fairy tales[16], as well as one that I wrote myself.

Again, I know what you're thinking: 'Fairy tales? But those are for kids! I need *useful* vocabulary, about business and science and technology. There's no way to make that fun!'

The thing with language is, there isn't such a big difference between Important Language and Fun Language[17]. We use a wide range of words when talking about technical topics as well as chatting with our friends.

A study by McQuillan[18] examined vocabulary in 22 novels and found that they included 85% of words on academic word lists. Rolls and Rogers[19] found that, if a student read a million words of science fiction, they would acquire many of the technical words required for a science degree.

So yes, reading fairy tales will help your English in all areas, even for academic purposes. As an English teacher, I've seen time and time again[20] that the students who do the best are those who read the most. For IELTS, for university, for business or just for travel, reading is the factor that predicts success.

But I understand if you're still unsure. When I learned about all this, I was, too. Thankfully, I like to experiment, and I have a passion for learning languages.

So in 2017, I decided to put this theory to the test[21]. I had wanted to learn Spanish for a long time, but aside from struggling with Duolingo[22] and not really learning anything, I hadn't made a serious attempt. I set myself a goal: I would read a million words in Spanish and see what my level was afterwards. A million words is roughly equivalent to twenty standard-length novels, so it was a huge task to undertake.

I started with very easy resources, like transcripts[23] of podcasts for learners, but I avoided anything that felt too much like work. Once I'd built up a solid foundation, I started reading translations of books that I knew in English, such as *Harry Potter* and *A Song of Ice and Fire* (you might know it as *Game of Thrones*).

Finally, I was ready to move onto completely new books, and I fell in love with Latin American[24] authors such as Isabel Allende, Luis Jorge Borges and Manuel Puig. Alongside the reading, I also listened to podcasts, but I always read the transcripts and counted the words as part of my reading.

After I hit my goal, I tested myself by writing and talking to native speakers, and found I was at a decent intermediate level. I could understand almost everything I read, understand clear speech, and converse[25] at a comfortable level, even though I had barely spoken the language since I started learning.

I had been learning for about a year, and I had made more progress than most students make in five years.

I didn't memorise[26] the vocabulary and grammar rules. I absorbed them.

By this point, you're either thinking, 'This is all

complete nonsense!' or you're super excited, ready to dive into[27] books and read for hours a day.

But the next thing I'm going to say is of utmost importance: **you must read books that are easy. You must read books that are fun[28]. If a book is too difficult or too boring, put it down and find another one.**

Stephen Krashen, an expert in the field of second language acquisition[29], says, 'Read only material in the second language that is genuinely fun and interesting, material that is so easy that you probably feel guilty reading it in your primary language. This is your excuse to read comics, magazines, detective stories, romances, etc. There is no shame in reading translations.'[30]

Ideally, you want to be reading a book so easy that, when you see a word you don't know, you can understand the meaning from context. Research has shown that in order for this to happen, the text needs to be at least 98% known words[31].

'98%? That's so high!'

I know, dear reader. But let me show you an example. Here's a text where I've replaced 10% of the words with nonsense words—that is, it's 90% comprehensible[32].

Jerry FLURGED out of bed and threw open the curtains. It was a beautiful day! He BIMPED to himself as he went about his daily routine, pouring coffee and buttering[33] POFFER. But then his phone rang, and the TORNGLER was so unexpected that he dropped his VINKY on the floor.

Is that easy to understand? Could you read a whole book of that?

WHY YOU MUST READ

Here's the same text, but 98% comprehensible:

Jerry jumped out of bed and threw open the curtains. It was a beautiful day! He sang to himself as he went about his daily routine, pouring coffee and buttering toast. But then his phone rang, and the caller[34] was so unexpected that he dropped his VINKY on the floor.[35]

How was that?[36] Even if you couldn't understand everything, I bet it was far more enjoyable to read than the first text. And that's the magic of reading for pleasure: even if you didn't understand everything, you got enough to follow the story and keep going, without having to pick up a dictionary!

So if you find that this book is too hard, put it down and read the level below. If you find it boring, go read something else. Yes, I'm giving you permission to stop reading my book. I know my writing isn't to everyone's taste, and that's OK. Find what works for you.

As you read, focus on the meaning of the stories, and don't sweat it[37] if you don't understand every single word. Just relax, and try to get lost in the pages. Believe it or not, when we have fun, we learn far better.

The levels of these volumes are based on the Common European Framework[38] of Reference, a system for defining language levels. You'll know them as A1, A2, B1, B2, C1 and C2, although these books only cover A2-C1. If you're A1 level, you probably need more guided teaching before you start reading, and if you're C2 level, then you can start taking on books for native speakers.

A great strategy, if you don't feel so confident about

your reading ability, is to start with the beginner level of the book and reread[39] it level by level. This will allow you to really absorb the new language and gradually increase the difficulty. There is not a huge difference between the intermediate-level stories and the advanced-level stories, but even rereading the same story twice can be very effective. We need to repeatedly encounter new words and phrases before our brain can really understand them.

Finally, this book has no exercises in it. I considered adding them after each story, but it would contradict[40] everything I just told you. The most effective way to spend your time is reading for pleasure, and exercises distract from that.

If, however, you finish this book and find yourself wanting more stories, do go and check out my podcast, *Easy Stories in English*. I publish a new story every week, with audio[41] and text, and there are over a hundred episodes for you to listen through.

Happy reading and happy learning!

-Ariel Goodbody

THE NORTH WIND AND THE SUN

Nature is a varied and wonderful thing. We have water, which we can drink from, swim and bathe in[1]. We have fire, which lets us cook food and keep warm. We have trees, which give us fruit and wood. All the parts of nature work in harmony, allowing us to live on Earth.

In particular, there are two very important parts of nature: the North Wind and the Sun. The former lets us know when the weather is about to change, and the latter keeps us warm and gives us light.

But the North Wind and the Sun work a bit differently to the other parts of nature. Instead of working in harmony, they constantly argue over which one is better than the other, and there is one matter on which they can never agree: what being strong actually means.

For the North Wind thinks that strength comes from power. If you have power, you can do what you want, and all must respect you or be crushed[2] under your thumb.

The North Wind sees how humankind goes to war and slaughters[3] each other, and therefore she knows that power is what makes you strong.

'The humans get it,' she says to herself. 'The strongest person is always the leader, and if anyone gets in their way, BAM[4]! It's over for them. Strength is power.'

The Sun thinks otherwise. She thinks that strength comes from kindness. If you are kind, everyone will like you, and in your time of need there will always be a friend there to help you. She sees how humans fall in love with each other, form families and close groups of friends, and therefore she knows that kindness is what makes you strong.

'The humans get it,' the Sun says to herself. 'Even if you are not the ruler of a country, the happiest humans are always the kindest. For when you are kind to the world, the world is kind to you.'

One day, the North Wind and the Sun were hashing out[5] their usual argument.

'You're just a little weakling[6], really,' said the North Wind. 'You have all that sunshine and heat, but you couldn't hurt a fly.'

'I don't need to hurt anyone, thank you very much.'

'Nonsense! What if all the clouds in the sky came to suffocate[7] you? Would you just sit there and die?'

'And why would the clouds attack me? They are my friends.'

'Just suppose! What if it happened? What would your kindness do for you then?'

'That's a ridiculous question, because it would never happen. Unlike you, I don't go around making enemies.'

'Ugh, you're unbearable!' said the North Wind. 'Fine, since I'm such a good friend, I'll help you understand. See that man down there?'

The Sun looked down at the earth, where a man was walking along a country road. It was winter, and there was a bitter cold in the air, so the man was wrapped tightly in his coat.

'Here's how it will go,' said the North Wind. 'We'll both try to make that man take off his coat. Whoever does it first wins. If you win, I'll admit that kindness is what makes you strong. But if *I* win, then you have to agree that power is what makes you strong. Got it?'

The Sun smiled. 'Fine. I will play your game.'

'Me first,' said the North Wind. 'This won't take long.'

The North Wind flew down to the man and blew as hard as she could. The trees started to shake, leaves flew through the air, and all the birds scattered[8]. An icy chill[9] came over the earth.

This person is holding their coat tightly because it is cold

But instead of removing his coat, the man held it tighter. The more the North Wind blew, the colder it got, and the tighter the man held his coat. No matter how hard the wind blew, the man would not take off his coat.

'Hmm!' said the North Wind, flying away with a

frown[10] on her face. 'I gave my all. If *I* couldn't get him to remove it, you certainly won't be able to. You might as well give up now.'

The Sun smiled. 'I think it's worth a try.'

She moved out from behind the clouds and bathed the world in light[11]. The trees stopped moving, the birds sat on their branches and sang, and the cold earth warmed up.

As the man walked, he started to break a sweat[12], and, seeing the Sun shining bright, he took off his coat and slung[13] it over his arm. He walked and whistled to himself, and eventually it was such lovely weather that he stopped and sat in the shade by a tree to enjoy it.

'I don't understand!' cried the North Wind in exasperation[14]. The Sun had just stood there!

The Sun laughed. 'I told you that strength comes from kindness. Who doesn't love a warm summer's day?'

The North Wind couldn't believe it. 'I still don't agree with you. You were just lucky. This guy liked the sunshine, but that doesn't mean all humans are stupid like that!'

The Sun smiled. 'We don't have to agree on everything, you know. I still love you.'

And the North Wind felt very warm and could say nothing more.

STRANGE FRIENDS

Once upon a time, there were a cat and a mouse who lived together in a little house. Unlike others of her kind, the cat did not chase and eat the mouse, which meant that they could be friends, and indeed they were[1]. Everyone called them the 'strange friends', and they lived a peaceful life in the city.

One day, the cat came and spoke to the mouse.

'We must think of winter. It is bright and sunny now, but in a few months' time it will be dark and cold, and there will be hardly any food to eat. We should save something for then. After all, if you go out looking for food in the winter, a cat might eat you!'

'You're quite right,' said the mouse. 'I know just the right food to keep. Let's buy a pot of fat.'

So they bought a pot, and were about to store it in the kitchen, when the mouse said, 'Wait! We cannot keep it here. If we see it, we will want to eat it. Let us put it somewhere where we will forget about it until we need it: in the church, under the altar². Out of sight, out of mind³.'

So they went into the church, hid the pot of fat under the altar, and then went home and promptly forgot about it.

Or at least, the mouse forgot about it, but the cat thought about the pot of fat very often.

At first she thought, 'Ah, what a wonderful idea it was to get that pot of fat! We will be very thankful for it in winter.'

But as the weeks passed, she thought more and more about the fat, and her thoughts began to turn selfish. She fantasised about⁴ going and eating the fat. It would taste so good!

So the cat came up with a plan. She came to the mouse and said, 'Dear mouse, I have to ask you a favour. You see, my cousin has given birth to a beautiful little kitten with white and brown fur. He really is very special, and my cousin has asked me to come to the christening⁵ and be his godmother⁶. As I'm sure you can understand, this is an honour. Would it be alright if I left you to look after the house alone, just this one day?'

'Of course, of course!' said the mouse. 'Family comes above all. Go and enjoy the christening, and if there happens to be some nice food or drink, bring a few crumbs⁷ back to me. In fact, I would love just a few drops of the wine—christening wine is always sweet and delicious.'

The cat smiled and said, 'I'll do my best.'

Naturally, the cat was lying. She had no cousin and nobody had asked her to be godmother. She happily strolled out of the house and went straight to the church, pulled out the pot of fat, and opened it up.

Oh, it looked so good! The cat licked at it, savouring[8] the delicious taste, and she ate the top layer of the fat, until she was quite full up.

Then she went for a walk on the roofs of the city. She hoped to spot some dessert there, but finding none, she lay down in the sun and had a nap. She fantasised about the pot of fat again, licking her lips in anticipation[9] of the next time she could eat from it.

When she returned home that evening, the mouse said, 'Well, you look like you've had a smashing time[10]! I suppose it was a good christening[11], then?'

'Oh yes, the best I've ever been to.'

'And what did they name the child?'

The cat thought for a moment and then said, 'Top-Off.'

'Top-Off!' said the mouse. 'I must say, I have never heard such a peculiar name in my life. Are there others in your family with that name?'

'It is a perfectly normal name, thank you very much. You have a godchild[12], don't you? He's called Big Nose, if I recall. That's just as strange a name as Top-Off.'

And with that, the conversation was over.

But the cat did not stop thinking about the pot of fat, and a week later, she was filled with the desire to eat from it again.

So once more, she went to her housemate[13] and said,

'My dear mouse, I'm afraid I must ask for your assistance again. My cousin has quite an active disposition[14], and has already given birth to another child. This one has a white ring around her neck, which is quite a rarity. They want me to be godmother again, and I am afraid I cannot say no. Would you be so kind as to look after the house one more time?'

'No problem, pal[15]! Go and enjoy yourself, and if you could possibly spare a few drops of that christening wine…'

'Oh, we drank it up so quickly last time! But I will try.'

Of course, the cat did not go to any christening, but to the altar in the church. This time, she ate half the pot of fat, filling her stomach up to bursting.

'Food tastes much better when you don't have to share it with anyone else,' she mused to herself[16].

Upon arriving home, the mouse of course asked her, 'What did they name the child this time?'

'Half-Done,' said the cat.

'Half-Done! Are you telling the truth? I have never heard of that name. I don't think you would find it in a single name dictionary in the country!'

'Then perhaps the dictionaries should be rewritten,' grumbled[17] the cat.

A few days later, the greedy cat got hungry again, and once more fantasised about[18] the fat. Well, if she had already gone this far, why not go further?

'Good things come in threes[19],' announced the cat to the mouse. 'I have been asked to be godmother again. This child is black with white hands, which, as I'm sure you can imagine, makes it really quite a special kitty[20]. I must attend the christening. Will you take care of the house while I'm gone?'

'Top-Off! Half-Done! Those names really do give me pause[21]. I wonder what name it will be today?'

'Well you just sit at home and wonder while I go and take part in the christening.'

So the cat headed off to the church. In the meantime, the mouse cleaned the house from top to bottom[22], while the cat ate the rest of the pot of fat.

'It is so good to finish a meal,' said the cat. She was so full that she had a long sleep on the roof and did not return home until the late hours of the night. The mouse eagerly asked what they had named the third child.

'You're not going to like this,' said the cat. 'He is called All-Gone.'

'All-Gone!' cried the mouse. 'Why, that is the strangest name of all! I have never heard such a name in my entire life. What could it mean?'

Pondering[23] these questions, the mouse went off to bed.

After that day, the cat's 'cousin' did not have any more children, and she was called to no more christenings. Winter finally came, and they ran out of food, but the mouse was not deterred[24] by this.

'It is a good thing we have that pot of fat!' she said. 'Let's go to the church and enjoy our food.'

'Yes,' said the cat to herself, 'although you might as well

stick your tongue out of the window and lick the air for all the good it will do you[25].'

'Hmm, what was that?'

'Oh, nothing! I am simply looking forward to our food.'

But when they arrived at the church, they found the pot empty.

'Oh no!' said the mouse. 'I see what has happened. I thought we were friends, but in fact you have betrayed me! While you were "going to christenings", you were really off eating the fat. First Top-Off, then Half-Done, then—'

'Do not finish,' said the cat gravely[26]. Just the sound of the names evoked memories[27] of the delicious fat, and she was getting *very* hungry. 'If you say another word, I'll—'

'All-Gone!' cried the mouse.

And with that, the cat jumped on her and ate her up.

Because that is the way of the world. Cats eat mice, and cats get fat.

THE VERY HUNGRY DRAGON

A dragon

Once upon a time, there was a very hungry dragon called Grella. Every day, she ate five massive meals. For breakfast she had ten bananas, five fried eggs, and three slices of toast. For her mid-morning snack[1] she had twenty chocolate biscuits and three cups of tea. For lunch she had twenty bowls of soup and thirty loaves of bread. After lunch, she always felt a bit sleepy, so she napped[2] for an hour, and upon waking up, she swallowed a whole jar of pickles, because she loved the salty taste. Finally, for supper she had a roast pig, dripping with fat[3] and covered with honey and herbs.

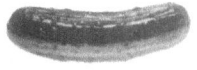

A pickle

This was all very well and good. After all, Grella was a dragon, and dragons are almost always hungry. But one thing was peculiar, and that was that Grella never ate jewels.

'I can't understand it!' said Grella's mother. 'Soup and pickles and pork are all fine, but you need some jewels in you! Jewels have important vitamins in them.'

But Grella hated jewels with a passion[4]. She found them hard and tasteless. At every meal, her mother pushed a plate of them at her, but she never took a bite. When her mother tried to force her, she hid them in her cheeks and spat them out[5] later. Her mother even tried disguising the jewels. She made a tomato out of rubies[6]. She made a cucumber out of emeralds[7]. She made an aubergine out of amethysts[8]. But Grella smelled them, recognised them for what they were, and threw them on the floor.

One day, Grella's refusal to eat jewels became too much for her mother.

'Grella, if you don't eat your jewels, then you can't have anything else.'

She took away the bananas, and the eggs, and the bread and the biscuits and the pickles. She filled every cupboard with fresh, shiny jewels, and for every meal the family would have nothing but jewels.

'Now, eat your dinner, Grella.'

Grella stared at the plate of emeralds in front of her. They were a horrible green colour, like vomit[9].

'I won't.' She flew to her room and slammed the door behind her.

For a few days, she continued in this way. She hid in

her room, ignoring the plates of jewels that her mother left outside her door. She thought that eventually her mother would get so worried that she would give in and bring her a nice juicy pig, but as the days passed, the jewels piled up and Grella got more and more hungry.

Finally, unable to restrain herself, she crept out[10] one night into the kitchen.

She picked up an emerald and stared at it. It just looked so *strange*. It looked like something you would put on your tail, or decorate your house with. Not something you would *eat*. But all the other dragons in the world ate them…

Grella's stomach rumbled[11]. She put the emerald in her mouth and took a cautious bite. It was so *bland*[12], but she had no choice. Slowly, she munched[13] and crunched[14], until the emerald turned into dust in her mouth. Then she swallowed it and went, 'Eugh!' Although it tasted bad, it did deal with her hunger, so she ate another, and then another.

By the next morning, Grella had eaten all the jewels in the house. Her mother was overjoyed[15].

'Wonderful, just wonderful! Wait here, Grella. I'll go out and fetch some more jewels for breakfast.'

Her mother brought three baskets of jewels back with her, stolen from some king's castle. It was enough to feed a whole family for a week, but while her mother went to wake up the rest of the family, Grella ate all three baskets, and licked her lips, waiting for more.

'Grella!' said her mother. 'You can't have eaten all

those jewels…?'

'I did,' said Grella. 'And I want more. Where's dessert?'

'Those were all the jewels I got!' said her mother. 'Look, I can go and make some toast if you want.'

But all Grella could think about was eating jewels. She needed more and she needed bigger, shinier ones. And most importantly, she needed them *now*.

Grella ran to the window and jumped off the balcony, spreading her wings and taking flight.

'Grella, where are you going?!' shouted her mother. 'It's a school day!'

But Grella didn't hear her. She flew through the air, and in the distance she smelled jewels. She followed her nose, passing over the rough, sharp mountains where they lived, until she came across a merchant road[16]. There, down below, was a cart from a faraway[17] land.

And it was laden with[18] jewels.

Grella was a well-educated dragon. She knew that it was bad to kill humans, because then they would come and get revenge. But that didn't mean she couldn't have a bit of fun.

She flew down and ripped the roof off the caravan[19]. The human merchants saw her and screamed, running away and abandoning their goods. Grella laughed, and picked up the caravan in her hand. She emptied it into her mouth, letting all the jewels pile up before she munched and crunched them into a delicious mixture and swallowed it in one go.

Grella understood now. Her mother had been right.

Jewels were *amazing*. They made her feel wonderful, like there was a party going on inside her stomach.

Grella gave a big, loud burp[20], and flew off to find more food.

Grella went wild for a whole week, flying round the world and stealing all kinds of jewels. Word quickly spread of her behaviour. Young dragons all around started copying her, leading to a wave of jewel theft that humans had never seen the likes of before[21]. Of course, all the adult dragons disapproved. She was giving them a bad reputation and putting herself in danger. Besides, she should really be in school!

Eventually, after eating so many jewels, she grew fat and heavy, and feeling satisfied, she flew home to hibernate[22].

But her mother had different ideas.

'Grella, HOW DARE YOU?!'

Grella blinked at her mother. 'Didn't you *want* me to eat jewels?'

'I— I— Not like *this*! I've been so worried about you, and besides, now everyone is talking about our family and saying nasty things. It was very inconsiderate[23] of you!'

Grella's mother kept shouting and telling her off, but Grella ignored her. She felt a deep exhaustion pass over her, and she couldn't stop herself from closing her eyes...

When she woke up, it was night. She had no idea how

long she had been asleep, but she was sure it had been a very long time. She knew this because her stomach was rumbling, which meant it was time to go and eat some jewels.

Grella crawled[24] to the kitchen, yawning loudly as she went. She opened the fridge.

No jewels there.

So she went and opened the cupboards.

No jewels there, either.

She looked in the freezer.

No jewels there!

She searched the entire house, and even crept[25] into her parents' bedroom to look around while they were asleep, but she couldn't find a single jewel anywhere!

She did find something in her brother's room, though. Under the bed he had a secret collection. He hated the all-jewel diet their mother had put them on, and he had hidden away all kinds of food: pickles and biscuits and chocolate and bread and tins of all sorts of soup. Grella pulled the food out, piled it up on the kitchen table and stared at it.

They didn't shine like jewels. They had odd smells. Some were hard, but some were very soft. They had all sorts of different colours. Cautiously, she picked up a chocolate biscuit and licked it.

Oh, how she had missed that taste!

Grella started to eat, and by the time her parents woke up, she had devoured[26] pretty much everything. She lay down on the floor and gave a big, happy burp.

'Oh, my daughter!' cried her mother. 'My daughter is back!'

She went and hugged Grella, pressing into her and making the young dragon feel sick.

'I don't understand you!' she said in annoyance. 'First you want me to eat jewels, then you shout at me for it, and now you're happy that I'm eating other food!'

'I know, I know. Please forgive me. I should've never forced you to change.'

She started crying, and hugged Grella even tighter. Honestly, mothers were so confusing!

'My food!' cried Grella's brother when he saw the remains of her feast. 'Grella, how could you?!'

'Don't worry,' said their mother, standing up and wiping her eyes dry. 'From now on, we will have *all* kinds of food in this house. There will be jewels for those who want them, and human food as well.'

And so everything went back to normal. Every day, Grella ate five massive meals. For breakfast she had ten bananas, five fried eggs, and three slices of toast. For her mid-morning snack[27] she had twenty chocolate biscuits and three cups of tea. For lunch she had twenty bowls of soup and thirty loaves of bread. After lunch, she always felt a bit sleepy, so she napped for an hour, and upon waking up, she swallowed a whole jar of pickles, because she loved the salty taste. Finally, for supper she had a roast pig, dripping with fat and covered with honey and herbs.

Oh, and she still ate the occasional jewel, just for variety.

DOGGO AND KITTY DO THEIR LAUNDRY

Once upon a time, there was a dog and cat, called Doggo and Kitty. Doggo was a very handsome dog, with long, thick fur that brushed along the floor, whereas Kitty was a charming and gorgeous cat, with soft, thin fur that felt like silk. The pair of them lived together in a little cottage next to a forest, but unlike most dogs and cats, they got on swimmingly[1].

Although Doggo and Kitty were only small little creatures, they had big dreams. They longed[2] to be like the Big People: the adults. Oh, how wonderful that would be! If only they could walk like adults, talk like adults, and live complicated, elegant lives like adults.

But alas[3], it was not meant to be[4]. Adults have hands, and Doggo and Kitty only had paws which, while soft, were big and clumsy. Instead of fingers that bent and wriggled[5], they only had sharp claws, which made it very difficult to do things as the adults did.

A paw (animal hand) with sharp claws (they can hurt you!)

And yet, Doggo and Kitty worked their hardest to be like the Big People, even if they failed. Perhaps you are wondering: if Doggo and Kitty weren't adults, did they go to school? The answer is no, of course. School is not for animals, but for children. Doggo and Kitty were neither adults nor children, but animals. Naturally, there was no way they could go to school, but they didn't mind this, because school seemed quite boring, anyway.

As previously mentioned, Doggo and Kitty lived in a little cottage, which was made of smooth wood and had a pretty red roof. The inside, however, was not so tidy, as Doggo and Kitty had to rule the household with only their clumsy paws, meaning things got messy very quickly. This was not helped by the fact that they loathed[6] cleaning.

One day, Doggo and Kitty were hunting for clothes to wear. They loved wearing shirts and trousers and hats, as it made them feel like adults. But alas! There was not a stitch of clothing to be found[7]. They were not in the drawers, nor in the cupboards or on the hooks.

'What is this nonsense, Kitty?' said Doggo. 'I think a clothes thief has snuck[8] into our house in the night and stolen all our clothes!'

'Not a clothes thief,' said Kitty, 'but rather a clothes *monster*. Oh, and I am so afraid of monsters!'

'Not to worry, Kitty!' said Doggo. 'I've found them.'

Instead of in their proper home, their clothes were lying on the floor, in a great, dirty, dusty pile.

'Well this simply won't do,' said Doggo, scratching his head. 'Our clothes are all dirty, and no decent adult wears dirty clothes.'

'You're absolutely right, Doggo,' said Kitty.

'So we will have to burn them and buy new ones,' said Doggo.

'No!' said Kitty. 'We should *wash* them.'

Doggo blinked. 'Ah, yes! The adults have a word for that, don't they? They call it "laundry".'

'Precisely,' said Kitty, and then got very excited. 'We are going to do our laundry, just like the adults do!'

'Fantastic!' said Doggo. 'But, er, how exactly *do* adults do laundry?'

'Oh, it's quite simple,' said Kitty, taking on the air[9] of a professor. 'You go and fetch some water, and I'll go get the soap and the washing board.'

'Alright then!' said Doggo.

So Doggo carried a bucket outside to the river, straining[10] under the weight, and then filled it with water. Meanwhile, Kitty searched through the kitchen cupboards. She found many odd things: toothpaste,

A woman using a washing board

lipstick[11] and even buttons. After all, the kitchen was the place for things that you put in or on your mouth, and Kitty did so like to chew on buttons. Finally she found what she was looking for: a round, red bar of soap that glittered[12] in the light. She carefully placed it on the table and then went off to find the washing board. After all, how could you do your laundry without a washing board?

When Doggo came back inside, sweating and heaving[13] under the heavy bucket, his eye was immediately drawn to something he saw on the table. He dropped the bucket with a PLOP and went to look at the shiny object, which was round and red and glittered in the light.

Well, thought Doggo, *seeing as[14] we are in the kitchen, this must be something to put in or on my mouth. And it looks very tasty indeed!*

And what do you do with tasty things? Why, you eat them, of course!

So Doggo put the red thing in his mouth and bit down on it.

But, oh! Eugh! Argh! It was not tasty at all! In fact, it was *revolting*[15]!

'Eugh!' cried Doggo, spitting out[16] the soap. 'This is horrible!'

As he coughed and spat, his mouth filled up with foam. The more he coughed, the more foam there was, until there was foam leaking out of his mouth and nose. Just at that moment, Kitty came back into the kitchen.

'Doggo, dear Doggo!' she said. 'What on earth is the matter? You're spraying foam like a fountain! Are you sick?'

'No!' coughed Doggo. 'I'm not sick. I found this red thingy here, and I thought it looked tasty, like a piece of cheese, or maybe some sweets. So I ate it, but *pagh*! It was a nasty, horrible thing, something that does *not* belong in a kitchen, and now my mouth is full of foam!'

'Doggo!' said Kitty. 'That wasn't food at all. It was *soap*! The very soap[17] we were going to use to do our laundry!'

'Well, no wonder it tasted so bad!' said Doggo. 'Why was it in the kitchen?'

*Foam (pronunciation **FOME**) coming out of a bottle of Coke*

'Well, one time, one of the children told me that he'd been very naughty, and his mother threatened to wash his mouth out with soap. I'd never thought it was something to put in your mouth—and I *certainly* don't think so now—but hearing that, I put it in here. Just to be safe.'

'Oh!' said Doggo, jumping up with glee[18]. 'You mean the adults put soap in their mouths, too? Well then, I was simply being mature, Kitty.'

'Whatever the case,' said Kitty, 'I shall have to go and fetch another bar of soap, and you are *not* to eat this one under any circumstances, understand? Now go and get some water and wash out your mouth.'

'Yes, Kitty,' said Doggo.

So Doggo went and washed out his mouth with water

from the bucket, after which he went and fetched more. By the time he had returned, Kitty was standing with the washing board and a fresh bar of soap. They were all ready to do their laundry, except one thing was still missing.

'Wait, Kitty!' said Doggo. 'We don't have a brush. How are we supposed to do our laundry without a brush?'

'That's a good question,' said Kitty. 'Without a brush, we won't be able to rub and scrub[19] our clothes, like the adults do.'

'Hmm,' said Doggo.

They sat down for a while and pondered[20] the problem. Then Kitty leapt[21] in the air.

'Doggo, I have the perfect solution! Brushes have long, thick hair. And *you* have long, thick fur. We'll use you as a brush!'

'What a fantastic idea!' said Doggo.

So Kitty sat down with the washing board, the bucket of water, and Doggo. She threw some dirty clothes onto the washing board, wet the soap in the bucket, and rubbed the clothes all over. Then she picked up Doggo and rubbed and scrubbed him on the clothes, until they disappeared under a mountain of foam. Finally, she dipped them in the water and washed the foam away.

Afterwards, they had a pile of clean, wet clothes, and a very dirty, wet Doggo.

'Kitty,' said Doggo, 'I have discovered a flaw in our plan. 'We don't have a towel to dry the clothes with, and on top of that, I'm far too wet to be of any use.'

'Hmm,' said Kitty.

They sat down for a while and pondered the problem. Then Doggo leapt in the air.

'Kitty, I have the perfect solution! Towels have soft, thin hair. And *you* have soft, thin fur. We'll use you as a towel!'

'What a fantastic idea!' said Kitty.

So Doggo sat down with the pile of clothes and Kitty. He threw the clothes on the washing board and towelled them off[22] using Kitty.

Afterwards, they had a pile of clean, dry clothes, but Doggo and Kitty were dripping wet[23] and absolutely filthy.

'Doggo,' said Kitty, 'if an adult saw us now, they would turn up their noses in disgust[24]! We have finished our laundry, but now we must wash *ourselves*!'

'Alright then, Kitty,' said Doggo. 'I'll wash you, and then you wash me.'

So Kitty climbed onto the washing board and Doggo lathered her up[25] with soap. She shouted 'Ow!' and 'Oof!' because Doggo rubbed her hard and his claws were razor sharp. When Doggo was finished, it was his turn, and he climbed onto the washing board. Once again, she lathered him up, and he shouted 'Ow!' and 'Oof!' because she rubbed him just as hard as he had rubbed her, and her claws were just as sharp.

Finally, they stood up and squeezed each other, letting out all the water onto the floor.

'Simple,' said Kitty. 'Now we just need to hang ourselves up to dry, just like the adults do with laundry.'

'Aha!' said Doggo. 'So that's what the washing line is for. I thought it was for swinging on.'

They went into the garden, where the washing line hung between the house and a big oak tree. They clambered[26] up the tree and onto the line, which they hung off by their claws. The sun shone bright and warm.

Clothes on a washing line

'The sun is shining on us, Doggo!' said Kitty. 'We'll be dry in no time flat[27].'

But as soon as she said the words, a huge raincloud came, and it started pouring down.

'It's raining!' shouted Doggo. 'Our laundry is getting wet! We must take it down!'

Quickly, they leapt off the washing line and dashed inside the house.

'Is it still raining?' asked Kitty, poking her head out[28] the door.

'It's stopped,' said Doggo, 'so let's hang up our laundry again.'

Once more, they clambered up the oak tree and onto the washing line. The sun shone on them, and they would be dry in no time flat!

But then the raincloud returned.

'It's raining!' shouted Kitty. 'Our laundry is getting wet! We must take it down!'

Quickly, they leapt off the washing line and dashed inside the house. Then the sun came back out, so they ran outside, but then it started raining again, so they ran back inside. They hung from the washing line, ran inside, and returned to the washing line until it was evening, and the sun had stopped shining.

By this point, they were both clean and dry, but bone-tired[29].

'Our laundry is done!' said Doggo.

They had conveniently forgotten about the actual laundry, which lay in a wet pile on the floor.

'What a day!' said Kitty. 'But Doggo, we did our laundry! We're one step closer to being adults!'

'There's nothing more to do than go to bed,' said Doggo.

And with the satisfaction of a hard day's work, they climbed upstairs and into their beds and quickly fell asleep.

DOGGO AND KITTY TEAR THEIR
TROUSERS

Once upon a time, there was a dog and cat, called Doggo and Kitty. Doggo was a very handsome dog, and Kitty was a charming and gorgeous cat. The pair of them lived together in a little cottage next to a forest, and unlike most dogs and cats, they got on swimmingly[1].

We have seen how Doggo and Kitty did their laundry, so we now know that Doggo and Kitty are *very* good at doing the housework. And there were always so many things to do! In fact, there was so much to do that Doggo and Kitty often sat around pondering[2] where to start, and then got distracted by a piece of cheese or a mouse. At any rate[3], the day after they did their laundry was Sunday, and Sunday is a day of rest.

That morning, Doggo poked his nose through the window[4], saw that the sun was shining bright and cheerful, and said, 'Kitty! It is a gorgeous day. Let's take advantage of the sunshine and go to the forest. What else could one do on a day like this?'

'I completely agree,' said Kitty. 'And what luck! We have done our laundry, and now we can wear our nice clean clothes to go out.'

So they dressed up in their finest clothes and headed outside.

'Oh, how I wish I had a parasol[5]!' said Kitty. 'The bright sun hurts my eyes so, and I would be such a pretty little kitty with a parasol. I am quite sure *nobody* has seen such a pretty kitty before!'

'It won't do you any harm to get a bit of sun,' said Doggo. 'We've been cooped up[6] inside all winter, and you're looking quite pale. Yes, some sun will do you good!'

And Doggo was right, for once. During the winter they sat by the fire and played games, and some days they didn't see the sun at all.

Still, Kitty did not like being criticised on her appearance, so she bit back[7].

'Well,' said Kitty, 'you should see how *you* look. Your ears are completely uneven, one sticking up and one hanging down! It's quite unacceptable to walk around with uneven ears.'

'Oh dear!' said Doggo, not realising that Kitty was trying to hurt his feelings. 'Thank you for letting me know, Kitty.'

Doggo adjusted his ears to make them presentable[8] and they continued on their way. While they walked, they spoke about what they would do in the forest. Oh, what

This dog's ears are uneven, not even. One is up and the other is down.

fun they would have! They were going to play all sorts of games, like hide-and-seek[9], which was Kitty's favourite—Doggo always lost. He would hide in a bush or a tree, but his ears always stuck out, making him quite easy to find.

As they walked, they came past a bush with a rabbit inside. When the rabbit turned and saw Doggo, he burst out laughing.

'Haha,' said the rabbit, 'look at that ridiculous dog! He has one ear sticking up and the other hanging down. Just like this.' And the rabbit moved his ears to imitate Doggo's. Doggo gaped[10], checked his ears and, sure enough, they were uneven again.

'That nasty little rabbit is laughing at you!' cried Kitty.

Doggo got angry and chased after the rabbit. He jumped into the bush, but the spry[11] little creature was far faster than him, and easily ran away.

'Oh, there are so many thorns in this bush!' cried Doggo, picking some out of his paws. 'I should never have chased after that stupid rabbit.'

'Did those thorns really hurt you, Doggo?' said Kitty. 'Or are you just looking for sympathy?'

'Yes, you're right. It didn't really hurt.'

Doggo sorted out his ears and they continued on their way. A few minutes later, they bumped into some of the children, who lived on the other side of the forest.

'Hello, Doggo and Kitty!' said the children. 'Since it's such a lovely sunny day, we all decided to go for a stroll in the forest.'

'Great minds think alike[12]!' said Kitty, proud of herself for using one of the phrases that the adults used.

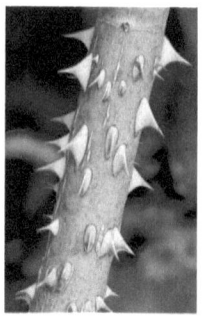
There are thorns on this rose. They are sharp and can hurt you.

'You're both dressed up nicely!' said the children. 'But, oh no!'

They started giggling[13]. Doggo quickly checked his ears, but they were even, so whatever was the matter?

'Look, boys! Look, girls! Doggo has torn his trousers!'

'What?!' said Doggo. 'Kitty, the *dear* children say that I have a tear in my trousers. Could you look and see?' Doggo didn't want to bend down and look himself, in case he tore them even more.

So Kitty took a good long look at Doggo's trousers, and then said, 'I'm afraid it's true, Doggo. Your trousers have a big tear in them.'

A needle and thread. You use them to make clothes.

'That must've happened when I ran into that bush with all those thorns!' said Doggo. 'Oh, I can't believe I've torn my nicest trousers. It's a crying shame[14]! But Kitty, perhaps you have a needle and thread?'

'I'm afraid I don't. But chin up[15], Doggo. I'm sure we'll

find something on the way, a piece of string or something like that.'

So they bid farewell[16] to the children, who were still laughing and pointing at Doggo, and continued on their way.

'Hey, take a look over there!' said Doggo. 'I spy something[17].'

There, lying on the ground, was a little worm, taking a nap in the afternoon sun. It was quite content, lying in the sun's rays, and it was confident that it was so small that nobody could see it. But it hadn't taken into account that there might be a dog searching for a piece of string.

'It's something long, thin and straight,' said Doggo. 'Why, I think it's a pencil!'

Hearing Doggo's booming voice[18], the worm woke up. When it saw the huge dog leaning over it, it had a fright, and curled up into a circle.

When you curl up, you move into this shape.

'No, Doggo, that's no pencil!' said Kitty. 'Pencils can't curl up into a circle. It must be a piece of string. What luck! I can use it to mend your trousers.'

And with that, Kitty picked up the worm and tied it in a knot to close the tear in Doggo's trousers. The poor little worm could do nothing to stop her.

'Fantastic,' said Doggo. 'Now nobody can laugh at me.'

They continued on their way and spoke about all the places they would hide in later when they played hide-

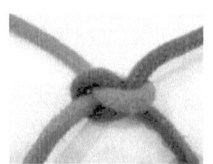
A knot
(pronunciation **NOT**)

and-seek. The worm listened and waited, and once it had recovered from its initial shock, it said to itself, 'I'm no piece of string! I'm a lovely little worm.' And, moving slowly so as not to bring attention to itself, it unravelled[19] itself.

Meanwhile, Doggo and Kitty came across one of their friends, Clucky the chicken.

'Hello, Clucky!' said Doggo and Kitty.

'Hello, Doggo and Kitty. Doggo, look out! There is something on your leg. Ooh, it's a worm!'

Being a chicken, Clucky *loved* to eat worms, so she pecked[20] at Doggo's leg and tried to eat it. Luckily for the worm, it had just finished unravelling itself, and it fell off and ran away before Clucky could catch it.

'How unusual,' said Clucky. 'It was climbing out of a hole in your trousers, as if it had been snacking on it. I didn't know worms ate trousers, but that's just one more reason for *me* to eat *them*. Shame I couldn't catch it. Then he really would have learned his lesson!'

'Yes, what a shame!' said Doggo. But secretly, he was relieved that Clucky hadn't caught the worm, as he hated violence.

'Oh, Doggo!' said Kitty, looking at his trousers again. 'Once again your lovely trousers are torn. That thing that ran away was not a worm, but the string I used to mend them!'

'No way,' said Clucky. 'That was a worm, no doubt

about it. String doesn't wriggle[21] and curl up like that! But there's no need to worry, Doggo. I can't mend your trousers myself, but if you follow this path along, you'll come to a house where a seamstress[22] works, and she can mend your trousers for you.'

So they bid farewell[23] to Clucky and continued on their way to the seamstress's house.

When she saw Doggo's trousers, she was taken aback[24].

'Wow, that's a big tear!' said the seamstress. 'But Sunday is a day of rest, so I don't really feel like working. I'll tell you what[25], if you help me out with a little problem, I'll mend your trousers for you. See, a family of mice has moved into my kitchen, and they're quite annoying, always stealing food and squeaking[26] in the night. If you get rid of them, I'll mend your trousers. *But*, you mustn't drink the milk or eat the biscuits laid out on the table! Those are for me.'

Doggo and Kitty agreed to catch the mice and promised to leave the milk and biscuits. The seamstress showed them to the kitchen, and all the mice ran away and hid in their holes.

'Here's the plan,' said Kitty. 'I'll go outside, and you stand in front of their holes, Doggo.'

So Doggo stood guard[27] outside the mice's holes. Kitty went outside and loudly said, 'Yay! There's a dog inside with one ear sticking up and the other hanging down, and he has a big tear in his trousers to boot[28]. How funny he looks! You can't help but laugh at him!'

The mice, who loved nothing more than a good laugh, ran out of their holes to see this funny-looking dog. And then, of course, Doggo jumped on them and caught them under his paw.

'Oh no!' cried the mice. 'Are you going to eat us? Oh, you do look so silly, but it's not worth dying for!'

'You're very lucky,' said Doggo, 'that I hate violence. But you must leave the seamstress's house and never come back!'

The mice promised to never return and ran away, giggling[29] to themselves about Doggo's trousers.

'Fantastic work!' said the seamstress, striding[30] back into the kitchen. 'A little unorthodox[31], but it got the job done. Now, let me have a look at those trousers.'

So the seamstress mended the tear in Doggo's trousers, and then she invited them to stay for milk and biscuits, and Doggo and Kitty couldn't say no to that, could they? The biscuits were quite delicious.

Afterwards, they walked home through the forest. In the end, they were too tired to play hide-and-seek, but they slept very well, although Doggo's ears were uneven throughout the night.

DOGGO AND KITTY BAKE A CAKE

Once upon a time, there was a dog and cat, called Doggo and Kitty. Doggo was a very handsome dog, and Kitty was a charming and gorgeous cat. The pair of them lived together in a little cottage next to a forest, and unlike most dogs and cats, they got on swimmingly[1].

One day, Kitty took a look at their calendar. It was five years out of date, but Kitty saw no reason to change it, because it wasn't as if each year was any different, was it?

'Doggo!' said Kitty. 'According to the calendar, today is my birthday.'

'Yay!' said Doggo. 'Birthdays are a wondrous[2] occasion. We will have to celebrate. But how? I have never celebrated a birthday before.'

Kitty was fairly sure they *had* celebrated a birthday before, since they happened every year. But she wasn't certain, because her memory often played tricks on her, and she didn't want to sound stupid. So she didn't comment on it.

'Yes, we must celebrate!' said Kitty. 'We'll have to think of the most wonderful and wondrous way to celebrate the most important birthday of all!'

While Doggo and Kitty pondered[3] the issue, so did another group of people: the children, who lived on the other side of the forest. They adored[4] Doggo and Kitty, and had missed Kitty's birthday last year, so this year they planned on surprising her with a cake.

The problem was, they had neither the ingredients for a cake, nor the knowledge of how to actually bake one. They were clean out of[5] flour, milk and eggs, and they weren't even aware that those were requirements for a good cake! After all, when you see a finished cake, you don't see the flour, milk and eggs. So they used whatever they had around and improvised[6] the recipe.

A cake tin and a cake

First, they found a battered[7] old cake tin, which they would bake the cake in. Then they took some sand from the sandpit[8] in the garden and poured it into the tin, because the best cakes were always soft, like sand. Still, it needed a bit of texture, so they poured in some water and mixed it with the sand, getting plenty of water and sand on the floor as they did so.

Now they had a lovely brown base cake, which only needed decoration to be perfect. So they took some small, white stones from the garden and placed them on top of it, because nice cakes always had nuts and things like that on top. Finally, they popped the cake tin in the oven and waited for an hour, although they oven wasn't switched on, because only their parents were allowed to do that.

Out of the oven came a most wondrous[9] cake! The children oohed and aahed[10] at it, and were very tempted to try it, but they knew that would be unfair. It was Kitty's cake, after all! So they carried it through the forest to the wooden cottage where Doggo and Kitty lived.

'Hello, Doggo and Kitty!' the children said. 'We baked you a cake and brought it here as a surprise for Kitty's birthday.'

'A surprise!' said Kitty. 'And not just *any* surprise. A culinary[11] surprise!' She had learned the word 'culinary' in a book, like the Big People were always reading, and she was very proud of herself for using it. 'Yes, culinary surprises are the best surprises of all. We were pondering[12] how to celebrate, and this is perfect!'

'The cake tastes divine[13],' said the children, copying the word their parents always used. 'You're going to love it.'

'Well then!' said Doggo. 'Come into the kitchen and we'll sit down to eat.'

But once they got a closer look at the cake, Doggo and Kitty soon realised that the cake was quite horrid[14]. What they had thought was a soft cakey texture was actually sand, and what they had thought were delicious nuts were actually stones. Nobody could willingly eat such a cake, but they adored[15] the children, so they cut up the cake—with difficulty—and served the slices around.

'You first, Doggo,' said Kitty. 'You're the oldest, so you get to eat first.'

'Oh no, I simply couldn't!' said Doggo. 'It's *your* birthday. You should eat first!'

So Kitty reluctantly held the slice of cake up to her nose and sniffed[16] it. It really smelled quite horrible, like earth and worms, so Kitty moved her lips, pretending to eat it.

'Yum yum!' she said. 'Oh, it's such a delicious cake, I don't think I could eat another bite!'

Doggo and the children soon understood the game. They all held up their slices, sniffed them and said, 'Yum yum!' and then put them down again.

'Thank you so much, children,' said Kitty, relieved she hadn't actually had to eat the cake. 'We've never had such a lovely cake before.'

The children laughed, said goodbye and headed home. Doggo and Kitty took the plates of cake to the river outside and threw them into the water.

'How nice of the children to do that for us,' said Doggo, 'but really, who could eat such a horrid[17] cake? Still, I am now very hungry for a *real* cake.'

'Me too,' said Kitty, her stomach rumbling[18]. 'Well, since it's my birthday, why don't we bake one? Although saying that, I don't actually know *how* to bake a cake.'

'I know, I know!' said Doggo, his tail wagging[19]. 'It's really quite easy, Kitty. All you have to do is add your favourite food to the cake. If you add five delicious foods, then the cake will be five times as good. If you add ten delicious foods, then the cake will be ten times as good.'

'What if we add a hundred delicious foods?' said Kitty.

Doggo chewed on his lip. 'Uh, I can't count that high! Maybe… a hundred times as good? Wow, that cake would taste really amazing!'

'Oh, this is marvelous!' said Kitty. 'We're going to make the most delicious cake ever!'

So Doggo and Kitty took out their cake tin, put on their aprons[20] and got to cooking.

First, they took flour, milk and eggs out of the cupboard and poured them into the bowl. Unlike the children, they had the basic ingredients, although they didn't know that you're not supposed to put egg shells in the bowl! They mixed furiously until they had a soft batter[21].

'Now what do we do?' asked Kitty.

'Now we add all our favourite things!' said Doggo. 'What kind of cake do you want to make?'

'Hmm,' said Kitty, 'well, above all, it must be sweet.'

So she poured a kilogram of sugar into the bowl.

'But not just sweet!' said Doggo. 'The Big People always like to have "balanced flavours".'

So he poured a kilogram of salt into the bowl, to make it even.

'And let's add some butter and jam,' said Kitty, 'since we always have that for breakfast.'

'*You* have jam,' said Doggo, 'but I like cheese on my bread. So let's add that instead.'

'Fine, fine,' said Kitty, 'but we need something greasy[22], too. How about bacon?'

'Perfect!' said Doggo. 'And let's not forget nuts. I really was looking forward to having the nuts on the children's cake, until I realised they were stones.'

'Nuts are fine,' said Kitty, 'but remember, Doggo! Balanced flavours! Let's have some cucumber, too.'

'And bones!' said Doggo, jumping and wagging[23] his tail in excitement. 'Oh my goodness[24], I can't eat a cake without bones! They're the best thing in the world!'

'Maybe for *you*,' said Kitty. 'But fine, if you're adding bones, I'm adding mice.'

'Oh,' said Doggo, 'if we're adding meat, pop in a few sausages, too.'

'And finally, cream!' said Kitty. 'Every good dessert has cream *on* it, but we'll make ours even better by having cream *in* it!'

'Fantastic thinking,' said Doggo, 'and I think that would go just right with a bit of garlic.'

'And chocolate,' said Kitty.

So they added all their favourite foods to the bowl, which happened to be all the food they had in the house. They mixed and mixed, sweating and heaving[25] over the mountain of food in the bowl, but finally, after hours of work, they reduced[26] it to a batter.

'Phew!' said Doggo. 'This is going to be an excellent cake. All we have to do now is bake it.'

So they carried the massive cake to the oven, careful not to drop it, and shoved[27] it inside. Unlike the children, they were allowed to switch the oven on, so their cake actually baked. While they waited, they left the filthy kitchen and went to play cards in the other room. When the cake was done, they took it out and put it on the table.

'Oh, what a handsome cake!' said Doggo.

'Not "handsome", Doggo,' said Kitty. 'Pretty! But we can't eat it yet, or we'll burn our mouths. We have to let it cool.'

So they opened the window and placed the cake on the windowsill[28].

'You know what?' said Kitty. 'Since the children were kind enough to bring us a cake, I think it's only fair if we do the same. But I don't want to carry it all the way through the forest.'

'No problem,' said Doggo. 'We'll invite them over here again.'

So they skipped[29] through the forest, thrilled at their baking success, all the way to the children's house.

But while they were away, a very naughty dog passed by the wooden cottage. The smell of the cake wafted[30] towards him, and his stomach rumbled[31] like a lorry.

'Why,' he said, licking his lips, 'I've never smelt something so delicious before. It's as if somebody mixed together a hundred delicious foods into one! I must find it.'

He followed his nose until he came across the cottage and saw the cake cooling. Oh, the cake looked just as good as it smelled! The dog's eyes and mouth began to water[32].

Without a moment's hesitation[33], the dog jumped onto

the windowsill and ate up the cake. The rumbling in his stomach went quiet, and he went to the river and drank lots of water. Then, feeling tired and satisfied, he sat down by a big tree.

Except he *didn't* feel satisfied. The cake had tasted so good going in, but in his stomach it felt so *bad*. It felt like he'd swallowed a hundred sticks and stones, or like there was a fire going on inside him!

'Oof! Ow! Just what was in that cake?' the dog asked himself.

When Doggo and Kitty returned with the children, they were horrified[34] to find the cake gone.

'Oh, no!' said Kitty. 'I am so sorry, children. I don't know what happened!'

'I think I know!' said one of the children.

He pointed in the direction of the river, where the naughty dog was sitting by a tree.

'That dog has a stomach as big as Mt. Everest[35]. *He* must have eaten the cake!'

The naughty dog would've gotten up and run away, except he was in too much pain.

'I'm sorry,' he said, hanging his head. 'It smelt so good, and looked so delicious, and I just couldn't stop myself! But oh, how I regret it!'

'Don't worry,' said Kitty. 'Judging by your reaction, the cake probably wasn't very nice in the first place. I have quite a delicate stomach, so I'm glad you ate it instead of us! Uh, no offence[36].'

'Well, I'm not glad!' cried the dog, and they all laughed.

'But there's just one problem,' said Doggo. 'We were going to have that cake for dinner, and we put all of the food in the house into it. Now we have nothing to eat, and I'm getting hungrier by the minute!'

'Not to worry, Doggo and Kitty,' said the children. 'Come and eat dinner at our house. We'll make mud pie for dessert!'

So Doggo and Kitty followed the children back through the forest to have dinner at their house. Luckily, their parents cooked, and made a lovely dinner of soup, chicken and bones. Doggo and Kitty were very happy to be able to eat with some of the Big People, and the food was delicious, too. Much better than sand cake and mud pie! Still, they didn't want to be rude, so they did as before and pretended to eat the children's dessert.

As for the naughty dog? Well, he was in so much pain he couldn't budge[37] an inch, and he sat up all night, whining[38] and crying as his stomach rumbled. But he learned his lesson. He would never steal from Doggo and Kitty again!

SLEEPING BEAUTY

A fairy is a girl with wings who can use magic

In a world far away from ours, in a time long past, there were two castles: the Blue Castle and the Red Castle. In the Blue Castle, where the fairies lived, everything was soft and blue as a clear sky. Joy ruled there, even when misery threatened it.

Among the fairies, one stood out as the most beautiful, a young creature called Izod. Izod loved her people, and her people loved her. She had a heart as soft as butter, and even the slightest injustice could bring her to tears. Whenever one of the High Fairies passed away, she mourned[1] for months longer than anyone else. Her softness of heart was only matched by the beauty of her wings, longer and paler than those of any other fairy. They shone in the sunlight and danced in the air as she flew, and everyone called them her 'wings of water'.

It came as a surprise to nobody when Izod was chosen to be the next queen. She was beloved[2] by all, and the ruler of the Blue Castle was always a fairy of great compassion[3]. At first, Izod was scared, but as the years passed, her excitement grew. On her sixteenth birthday, she would become queen, and she would be able to share all the love for her people that lived in her heart.

But on the day of her sixteenth birthday, the men from the Red Castle came.

Dressed in deep red, their eyes burned like the fires of hell. They dyed[4] the Blue Castle red with blood. They murdered without care, and for every drop of blood spilled Izod shed a bitter tear. When they finally came to her, her home lying in flames around them, her body was a dry, empty shell.

But the Red Men did not kill her. That would have been far too kind a fate for a fairy like Izod. They beat her, ripped out her wings, and left her alone in the Blue Castle. All alone.

Her beauty was dead, and her magic was gone.

Della loved her people, and her people loved her. Her mother and father, the King and Queen of the Red Castle, boasted loudly of her with pride, and her people gave her endless gifts and compliments[5]. She had gorgeous red hair, which burned bright in the sun, and the people called it her 'hair of fire'.

In the Red Castle, everything was warm, bright and strong, and Della was the strongest of all. She watched countless battles between gladiators[6] without fear, and when they killed each other, she jumped and cheered. She would be queen one day, and she would be a powerful queen.

But on Della's sixteenth birthday, everything changed.

The day started with beautiful sunshine but quickly turned dark and wet. Many people had come to celebrate the Princess's birthday, and now they stood packed inside the chilly castle, their bright mood ruined by the bad weather. It was an omen[7], said some, but the King and Queen laughed off their comments.

'The gods are simply afraid of your strength,' said the King, 'and even they wish to challenge you.'

Della smiled. 'One day, I will destroy them, too.'

Della sat on the throne[8] and received the people's gifts one by one: cakes, fine jewellery, gorgeous paintings and dresses, but most importantly, a wide range of weapons, and even a few war horses. Finally, Sir Galen, the head of the Queen's guards, came up, dressed in his autumn-leaf uniform. He had a particularly interesting present for Della, presented in a small wooden chest[9].

'These are fairy wings, Your Majesty[10]. They possess strong magic. Although it is a dangerous force, a powerful queen must learn to use all forces for herself. Be cautious with them.'

SLEEPING BEAUTY

Della reached forward to examine the wings, but as soon as she touched them, the doors to the Red Castle flew open, banging loudly against the walls. A howling wind[11] blew and sheets of rain swept inside, bringing cries of anger from the guests.

'Shut those doors!' commanded the Queen.

The guards attempted to do so, but the doors were held open by the force of the wind. Out of the rain stepped a tall figure wrapped in a black cloak. As soon as they were inside, the doors slammed shut behind them. All stood in silence and observed the mysterious figure, who pushed through the crowd towards the Princess.

A cloak (pronunciation CLOKE) is a big piece of clothing that you wear outside

'Who are you?' demanded the Queen.

The figure stopped and pulled off her hood. It was a woman, but no ordinary woman. Her skin was dark blue, covered with deep wrinkles[12], and her eyes were as white as milk. Despite her appearance, she had a softness about her, underlined by a great sadness. She looked like a rain-cloud personified[13].

Della had heard of the Blue Castle and the strange blue fairies who lived there, but they had all died, many years ago. That was what her parents had told her.

The blue woman raised a bony[14] finger and pointed at Della. 'Those wings are mine. Return them to me.'

Her voice came out as a dry whisper, but nobody else dared say a word as she spoke. For the first time in her life, Della felt fear, true fear.

'These are not your wings,' she declared. 'Sir Galen gave them to me.'

The blue woman repeated herself. 'Those wings are mine. Return them to me. I need them to fly.'

'Guards!' shouted the King. 'Capture this woman!'

But the guards stayed perfectly still, as did everyone else in the room. Under some kind of spell[15], no-one could move an inch, apart from the fairy and the Princess.

The blue woman repeated, stronger this time, 'Return my wings to me! I need them to fly.' She sounded like she might burst into tears at any moment.

Della calmly stood up, taking the wings in her hands. She held them up to the light and examined them. They were a beautiful piece of work, too intricate[16] and regular to be a work of nature, but equally, too thin and delicate to be the work of a human.

Della never gave things up without a fight. That was what her parents had taught her. And yet, she had a strange feeling in the pit of her stomach[17]. She knew that if she did not return the wings to this woman, her birthday would be ruined.

All eyes glaring[18] at her, Della descended the steps and went towards the fairy.

'No!' shouted Sir Galen. 'It is Izod, the wicked[19] queen of the Blue Castle!'

Della stopped suddenly. The fairy's face changed,

filling with anger. She jumped towards the wings, and her spell was broken[20]. The guards ran forward, grabbing her thin arms and easily holding her back.

'If she will not give me my wings, then let her suffer like me! If I cannot fly, then she must sleep. Tonight, your beloved[21] princess will fall into a deep sleep and never wake up again!'

And then, in an explosion of raindrops[22], Izod was gone. The damp cloak fell to the floor and left the guards grasping at air. The Red Castle fell silent, and the rain outside stopped, the sun finally returning. But none could feel its warmth.

Although the people of the Red Castle dismissed magic and those who used it, they understood its power. Nobody doubted the words of the blue fairy, and the King and Queen sought[23] the help of the best healers[24] and magicians[25] in the land to remove their daughter's curse[26].

But none could undo it, for it was a curse more powerful than any of them had ever seen. All they could do was take precautions.

So that night, Della did not go to bed. Neither did she the night after that. For a whole week, she avoided her bed as if it might burn her, and stayed awake by any means possible. Her parents found entertainers—musicians, clowns and dancers—to keep her occupied every minute of the night.

And yet, with each passing day, Della grew more tired, and her parents could do nothing about it. One night, while eating dinner together, her head fell onto her plate and she fell fast asleep[27].

The King and Queen tried to wake her up. They shook her violently. They waved sweet-smelling flowers and foul-smelling potions[28] in front of her nose. They had the musicians play as loud as they could. They held her nose and poured buckets of water over her. But the Princess did not move, and finally, exhausted and heartbroken[29], they carried her to bed. They sat by her every night, telling stories and brushing her hair. But eventually, their suffering grew too much, and even they left her.

Della lay alone in her room. She was a sleeping beauty, and nothing more.

Izod, too, slept. Without her wings, her magic was weakened, and the only way she could keep Della in her slumber[30] was to link it to her own.

In their dreams, the two girls met. At first, Della ran away at the sight of the fairy, escaping into the endless dimensions of the dreamland. But as the years passed—and she had no way of keeping track of the time—she realised that they would have to talk, sooner or later. So she sat down by the sea and waited, and eventually Izod came to her.

'Why did you do this?' Della asked. She no longer sounded like a proud child. She was a suffering woman now, just like Izod.

'I had nothing left.'

Della shook her head. 'But what did you gain from this? Now we are both asleep. You do not have your wings, and I will never rule my kingdom. Does it make you happy to see me suffer?'

'Of course it doesn't. I know how you are suffering. I feel your pain.'

Della bit her lip in a vain attempt[31] to hold back the tears that she had locked within her all her life. 'Then why did you do this?'

Izod simply raised a hand up. Out of the sea, two castles formed, one blue, one red. Watery[32] figures poured out of the Red Castle and marched towards the Blue, striking it with arrows and swords, smashing it to seafoam[33].

'I know the history of our lands,' Della admitted. 'I know it was wrong. But being queen is not easy. My mother has to do many things she doesn't want to do. And your people were dangerous. You had magic.'

'We all had magic, once.' Izod smiled. 'But they did not tell you that part of the story, did they? Once, we were all one, Blue and Red together.'

'What happened?' whispered Della.

'We broke ourselves up and killed our other half. Split ourselves in two.'

Della shook her head. 'Why?'

'For the same reason that my people feared yours and your people despised[34] mine. Unity never lasts. It is nature's way to split and divide. Animals kill each other, the sea tears apart[35] the land, and queens conquer.'

'Then why fight?' Della knew she was being selfish, but why couldn't the fairy leave her kingdom alone? Even if war was inevitable, couldn't her people be happy?

'Della,' said Izod, putting a hand on the girl's shoulder. 'There is one last hope. A way for us to wake up and bring our peoples back together. But you will not like it. You won't be able to go back to your life in the sun. That castle has crumbled down[36].'

Della stared into the fairy's eyes, deep pools of water. She had no reason to trust her. She was every part[37] the monster that her parents had warned her of. And yet, her parents were just as much monsters themselves. She saw that now.

'Tell me.'

Della woke up with a start[38]. No, she was not Della now. She was Izodella. She had her wings of water and she had her hair of fire.

A crack in a glass

Izodella floated out of bed and examined the dusty room she was in. Death and dirt had climbed into every inch and crack of the castle, and she knew instantly that her parents were gone. Many years had passed, and when she looked out of the window, she saw a dying land. The earth was Red, red with fire and blood, and she saw no joy or bravery, only misery and pain.

Without hesitation[39], Izodella flew to the throne[40] room, and there, sitting upon a throne twice as large as himself, sat Sir Galen.

'Well, well, well. The Princess has finally decided to wake up.' His face turned into a lustful[41] smile. 'I think I preferred you asleep.'

The King's—the new King's—guards rushed forward, but Izodella was faster than them. She dove[42] forward, pushing her nails into Galen's chest and ripping out his heart. The King gave his last breath and collapsed onto the floor.

Then came the guards and the soldiers. They swung at her with swords, fired arrows, beat her with sticks. She tossed them all aside[43] like flies, breaking through the castle doors and flying above it.

Below her, the people sweated and bled for their kingdom, and now they looked up at her with an expression of resignation[44]. The end had come, and they knew it.

Izodella raised her right hand.

Fire rained down. It swallowed the Red Castle and ran across the land, burning through fields and forests. It climbed mountains and danced across rivers, and finally it reached the ruins of the Blue Castle, devouring[45] them just as it had the Red.

Izodella raised her left hand.

Water rained down. It washed away the ashes[46] of the

fire, swept the bodies of the dead into the sea, and cleansed[47] the land.

Finally, the fire died and the rain stopped. The land slept. Izodella lowered her hands and cried. She cried rivers and oceans, her tears pouring onto the dry earth. All around, silence and darkness ruled.

And then, where her tears had fallen, something arose out of the dark, something this land had not seen for a very long time.

Green.

ONE-EYED, TWO-EYED, THREE-EYED

There was once a horrible old woman who had three daughters. The eldest daughter had three eyes, so she was called Three-Eyed. The youngest daughter had one eye, so she was called One-Eyed. The middle daughter had two eyes, so she was called Two-Eyed. Three-Eyed was beautiful, and One-Eyed was very clever, or so she liked to think, but Two-Eyed was ugly and of average intelligence. She was, however, very hardworking. Her sisters despised[1] her because she had two eyes like normal people, and her mother despised her because she was not special like her sisters.

One day, the old woman decided it was high time her daughters get married.

'Three-Eyed will marry a rich businessman, since she is so beautiful. One-Eyed will marry an academic, since she is so clever.'

'And who will I marry, Mother?' asked Two-Eyed.

'Foolish girl!' she cried. 'You will not marry anyone. You will stay at home and look after your dear mother.'

So the old woman prepared her eldest and youngest daughters for marriage.

First, she painted a second eye onto One-Eyed's face, so that it looked like she had two eyes. However, as One-Eyed's real eye was in the centre of her face, the second eye was off to the side, and it looked very funny indeed.

After that, she took some horse hair and made a fringe[2] to put on Three-Eyed's head, so that her third eye could not be seen. However, Three-Eyed had huge eyelashes, and they got caught in the fringe[3], making it look very untidy.

'There!' said the mother. 'Now, who wouldn't want to marry you?'

A few days later, a suitor[4] came to the house in search of a wife.

'I have searched far and wide[5],' said the man, 'and what I seek is an honest, hard-working wife.'

'Come in, come in!' said the old woman, ignoring his words. Men said they wanted honesty, but really they sought[6] beauty. 'Perhaps you would like to marry my eldest daughter, who is very pretty?'

The suitor looked at Three-Eyed and said, 'Hmm, I think not.'

Ah, thought the old woman, *he is one of those men who prefer intelligence to beauty, because they worry that their wife will go off and sleep with another.*

'Well, perhaps you would prefer my youngest daughter? She is very clever.'

The suitor looked One-Eyed up and down and said, 'I believe she's not my type[7]. Where is the middle daughter?'

'Oh no, she is ugly and stupid. You do not want to marry her.'

Two-Eyed was hiding in the next room. She had seen the man through the window, and found him very handsome. She wouldn't let her mother prevent her from having a chance to talk to him. She was allowed that, wasn't she, just to say hello? So she walked into the room and smiled at him.

'Hello,' she said.

'Ah! *This* is the daughter I want to marry. I can tell just by looking at her.'

'No, no!' said the mother. 'She does not want to get married.'

'But Mother, I—'

'Goodbye!'

And the old woman pushed the suitor out of the door and shut it. Suddenly, she, Three-Eyed and One-Eyed all turned on Two-Eyed.

'You think you're so clever, don't you?' said the mother. 'You cannot get married, you worthless brat[8]. I already told you.'

'Ugly girl!' said Three-Eyed.

'Stupid girl!' said One-Eyed.

Two-Eyed burst into tears and ran to her bed.

Meanwhile, the mother and the two favourite daughters thought about what to do. Three-Eyed suggested they kill Two-Eyed. That way, they would have a sob story[9] to tell the suitors, and what man wasn't attracted to a woman in distress?

But their mother shot the idea down[10].

'Don't be silly,' she said. 'I need Two-Eyed to look after me after you go and live with your rich husbands. No, we cannot kill the girl, but we must make sure no man will ever want to marry her.'

'Hrmm,' said One-Eyed, 'we could make her work very hard so that she is rough and unattractive.'

'I have a better idea!' said the mother. 'We will starve[11] her and overwork[12] her. Every day, she'll toil away[13] in the fields, and afterwards we'll give her just *crumbs*[14] to eat. She'll turn thin and hard, and nobody will want to marry her!'

'Great idea, Mum!' said One-Eyed. 'I wish I'd thought of that.'

So early the next day, Three-Eyed and One-Eyed pulled Two-Eyed out of bed, and told her she had work to do in the fields.

'What about breakfast?' she asked.

'No breakfast for you, lazybones[15]!' cried Three-Eyed.

So the girl went to the field and started working, watching the sun rise as she did so. It was a beautiful day, and she did not mind working hard, because her lunch would taste even better afterwards.

A few hours later, a goat came up to her.

'Meeeh! Good day, Two-Eyed.'

'How do you know my name?' the girl asked. 'And, oh! How can you talk?'

'I am no ordinary goat and you are no ordinary girl.'

'Oh, but I *am* ordinary. I am not beautiful like my older sister, and I am not clever like my younger sister. And I only have two eyes, just like you and everyone else.'

'Oh no, you are special. You merely do not know it yet. But that's not important. I bet you're hungry.'

'Yes,' she admitted, 'I am a bit peckish[16]. But when I finish working we'll have lunch, I'm sure. Oh, I'm so hungry I could eat a goat! Uh, no offence[17].'

The goat shook his head. 'None taken[18]. But there is no delicious meal waiting for you at the end of your labour. Your wicked[19] mother has a nasty plan. She intends to only give you the crumbs[20] of the other girls, and having watched them eat, I think they will leave very few crumbs indeed. They are trying to starve[21] you.'

'Oh!' said the girl, quite shocked. Her mother had never been particularly kind, but she had never been so *wicked*, either.

'But do not worry, my dear girl. As I said, I am no ordinary goat. Say these magic words and I will help you: "Little goat, little goat, it's time to eat." When you are done, simply say, "Little goat, little goat, it's time to go."'

The girl raised an eyebrow. She was starting to think that it might not be the best idea to trust this strange talking goat. But equally, she had nothing to lose, so she said, 'Little goat, little goat, it's time to eat.'

Suddenly, the goat transformed. His back stretched

A pickle

out into a long, white rectangle, and his fur morphed[22] into a tablecloth. All kinds of food appeared: bread, cheeses, jams, pickles, tomatoes, olives, and so on and so on.

'Oh my!' said the girl. 'Does that hurt?'

'Not at all,' said the goat, 'but mind that you don't spill jam on my back. It's a nightmare to clean off.'

The girl was feeling famished[23] from the work, so she devoured[24] the food in front of her, and when she was done, she said, 'Little goat, little goat, it's time to go.'

The table morphed back into a goat and smiled at her.

'See you tomorrow, Two-Eyed!' he said, and ran off into the distance.

'I wonder what his milk tastes like,' Two-Eyed murmured[25] to herself.

When she finished her work and came home, lunch had already been made and eaten. Judging by the smells and stains on the table, they had eaten a meal very similar to hers, although she was sure the food had not tasted half as nice as the goat's.

'I suppose you want to eat?' said the mother. 'Well, there are some breadcrumbs here, and a bit of cheese there…'

'No, thank you!' said Two-Eyed cheerily. 'I ate plenty of food yesterday.'

Her mother frowned[26]. 'Are you quite sure, Two-Eyed?'

ONE-EYED, TWO-EYED, THREE-EYED

'Absolutely! You know me, I don't need to eat much.'

For several days, this pattern continued. The mother and her two favourite daughters sent Two-Eyed into the fields to work, and she ate her fill[27] from the goat's back, politely refusing the crumbs she was offered at home. This sent the three wicked women into a frenzy[28], as they could not fathom[29] how Two-Eyed had not collapsed from hunger.

Finally, the mother cried, 'Enough! Tomorrow, One-Eyed will accompany Two-Eyed into the field and find out what's going on. The brat[30] is probably stealing food from a farmer.'

So the next day, One-Eyed followed Two-Eyed into the fields.

'Why are you following me?' said Two-Eyed. 'Are you going to help me with the work?'

'Eugh, no way!' said One-Eyed. 'I'm just so *bored*, and I thought it might be fun to watch you toil away[31] while I lie on the grass.'

So Two-Eyed laboured in the field, and when she took a break, she sat down on the grass next to One-Eyed. At one point, when they were very young, they had liked each other. One-Eyed used to put her head in Two-Eyed's lap and have her sing to her, and sometimes Two-Eyed missed those days.

'Oh, sister,' she said. 'Put your head in my lap and I'll sing you a song.'

One-Eyed scowled[32], but she did as Two-Eyed said.

'Sister, sister, are you asleep?

The goatherd[33] dances, the old man weeps[34].

Sister, sister, are you awake?

Let the day take you and cure all your aches.'

'I am awake,' said One-Eyed.

Two-Eyed repeated the song. She used to do this often with her sister, when she couldn't sleep at night.

'Sister, sister, are you asleep?

The goatherd dances, the old man weeps.

Sister, sister, are you awake?

Let the night take you and cure all your aches.'

'I am awake,' said One-Eyed, yawning loudly.

Two-Eyed continued to sing, making her voice quieter and quieter, until finally One-Eyed's eye closed and she started to snore. Then, Two-Eyed got up, making sure not to wake her sister, and went and found the goat, who was waiting not far away.

'Little goat, little goat, it's time to eat!'

The goat transformed into a table once more, and the girl ate her fill while her sister slept soundly[35]. Then she said, 'Little goat, little goat, it's time to go!'

The goat shifted back into his regular form and skipped[36] away, and Two-Eyed went and woke her sister.

'Come on, sister! It's time to go home.'

'Oh!' said One-Eyed, rubbing her face blearily[37]. 'Did I sleep for that long?'

That evening, the wicked mother and Three-Eyed asked One-Eyed what she saw, but the girl informed them she had fallen asleep.

'You stupid girl!' cried her mother.

'But I did see one thing,' One-Eyed said, her lip trembling. 'When she woke me up, she had some cheese on her mouth.'

'Hmm.' The mother stroked her chin. 'Tomorrow, Three-Eyed, you will go with her to the fields to further investigate. And don't make such a stupid mistake as your sister!'

So the next day, Three-Eyed tagged along with[38] Two-Eyed for her daily labour. Naturally, she was just as workshy[39] as her sister, so she lay down in the grass and watched Two-Eyed smugly[40] until lunchtime.

Two-Eyed had never put Three-Eyed's head in her lap and sang her songs, but she knew her older sister had been secretly jealous of this ritual[41] with One-Eyed. So Two-Eyed casually suggested they do the same.

'Pah!' said Three-Eyed. 'As if I would do something as childish as that.'

'Just for a moment, sister.'

'Fine. But only to show you how stupid it is.'

So Three-Eyed laid her head in Two-Eyed's lap and the girl sang to her.

'Sister, sister, are you asleep?

The goatherd[42] dances, the old man weeps[43].

Sister, sister, are you awake?

Let the day take you and cure all your aches.'

'Of course I'm awake,' said Three-Eyed. 'I'm not a baby.'

Two-Eyed repeated the song.

'Sister, sister, are you asleep?

The goatherd dances, the old man weeps.

Sister, sister, are you awake?

Let the night take you and cure all your aches.'

'I don't fall asleep that easily,' said Three-Eyed, yawning as wide as a door frame.

Two-Eyed continued to sing, making her voice quieter and quieter, until finally Three-Eyed's eyes closed and she started to snore. Then, Two-Eyed got up, making sure not to wake her sister, and went and found the goat, who was waiting not far away.

But actually, Three-Eyed was *not* asleep. She only pretended to snore, and closed her two lower eyes. But her third eye, hidden under the fringe[44], she kept open. Carefully, she rolled over, moved aside the fringe, and watched what Two-Eyed was doing.

'Little goat, little goat, it's time to eat!'

Three-Eyed observed the goat transform into a table, and she saw Two-Eyed eat a hearty[45] meal. No wonder the girl had rejected the crumbs they'd offered her! Then Two-Eyed said, 'Little goat, little goat, it's time to go!' and the goat returned to his usual form.

That evening, Three-Eyed feverishly[46] explained what had happened to her mother and sister. The old woman had never looked so happy in her life. She smiled so wide her whole face turned into wrinkles[47].

'She is a witch[48]!' said One-Eyed, her mouth wide open. 'We must tell the town and burn her.'

'No!' said the mother, slapping her hand. 'I need

someone to do the work here. Besides, that girl is far too plain to be a witch. I have a much better idea. I think tonight we will have goat curry for supper...'

'Yes,' said Three-Eyed, 'but what about the *magic* goat?'

'My dear, stupid girl. We are going to *eat* the magic goat.'

'Oh.'

Two-Eyed had been eavesdropping[49] through the door, and when she heard this, she burst into tears, and could not stop crying all day. That evening, she could not bear going down to supper, so she went to bed instead. She fell into a deep but troubled sleep, where she dreamt.

In the dream, she was toiling away in the fields. In the distance, a goatherd danced madly in the sun, but the magic goat did not come to visit her. Instead, an old man came to her in the moonlight, his face strewn with tears[50].

'Your family is planning on eating our friend, the dear goat.'

'I know,' said Two-Eyed weakly.

'Do not worry, my child. Leave the crying to me. We cannot save your friend, but we can make sure his sacrifice is not in vain[51]. After the meal is finished, take the goat's hooves and horns and plant them behind the door. Make absolutely sure that nobody sees you.'

*Some animals have hard feet called hooves (singular **hoof**)*

The girl nodded, and woke up. It was late evening, and

she could hear the raucous[52] laughter of her mother and sisters from the kitchen.

'Two-Eyed!' screamed One-Eyed. 'Come and watch us eat!'

Reluctantly, Two-Eyed climbed out of bed and went into the kitchen. There, the family was eating a delicious-smelling goat curry, rich with spices. Two-Eyed felt sick, but she had to stay and watch them eat every last drop. Still, she resolved[53] to not cry.

Some animals have sharp things on their heads called horns

After the meal was finished, her mother waved her hands at the pot and the plates and said, 'Clean up this mess, Two-Eyed.'

Two-Eyed waited for them to start snoring, and then took the hooves and the horns from the bottom of the pot. She dug a hole behind the door, working slowly and quietly, and planted the hooves and horns inside. Exhausted and distraught[54], she went to bed.

The next day, Two-Eyed woke up and saw leaves outside of the window. That was funny. There was no tree there. She went and saw that, where the hooves and horns had been planted, a beautiful apple tree had grown. And it was no ordinary apple tree; the apples were made of shining gold!

'Daughters, daughters!' cried the mother. 'It is a miracle!'

The old woman rushed outside as fast as her bony[55] legs could carry her, but as much as she tried, she could not pick an apple. Each time, the branches of the tree moved away, as if taunting[56] her. As Three-Eyed was the tallest, she was commanded to pick some, but the branches shied away[57] from her hands as well. They tried putting One-Eyed on Three-Eyed's shoulders, but the branches swung dramatically upwards, and they both fell onto the ground.

'It's not fair!' cried One-Eyed. 'Those are *our* golden apples!'

Two-Eyed, meanwhile, had cautiously come outside to watch. She stood in the door frame and marvelled[58] at the beauty of the apples. Her mother gave her a stern[59] look and said, 'Don't even think about trying to steal any for yourself, or I'll tell the town that you're a witch[60].'

'Yes, mother.'

But later that day, when they were taking a long nap after lunchtime, Two-Eyed reached for the tree. Unlike for her sisters, the branches actually bent down to meet her, and she plucked[61] the apple off the tree with ease. She stared at the beautiful apple for a while, mesmerised[62] by its shine, before hiding it in her dress and getting back to work.

A few days later, the suitor from before came round again.

'Have you had any time to reconsider my offer?' he said to the old woman. 'I've met many beautiful girls, but I still have my sights set on⁶³ your middle daughter. Are you quite sure she does not want to get married?'

'Yes, yes!' said the mother. 'She despises⁶⁴ the idea. Absolutely hates it. But it does not matter. The horrible little creature ran away.'

In fact, Two-Eyed was lying under her bed, where her mother had forced her to hide.

'Oh, what a beautiful tree you have!' said the man. It reminded him of a dream he'd had… 'Those apples glitter⁶⁵ as if they were made of gold. How on earth did you grow such a thing?'

'We simply looked after it well. Now, would you like to see my eldest daughter again? She really is very beautiful. Far better than my ugly middle daughter.'

The man thought for a moment, as he surveyed the glittering golden apples. True, beauty was far from the most important quality in a wife. But his father had been badgering⁶⁶ him to get married, and if he found a beautiful wife, then people think he was handsome, too. It was only such a shame that the middle daughter had disappeared!

If he were to marry someone he did not love, she would need to be hard-working. He wasn't sure if One-Eyed or Three-Eyed had ever lifted a finger in the house, so he decided to test his potential wives.

'Would your lovely daughters be able to pick me some apples? If they can find me a particularly golden and juicy apple, I think I might marry one of them.'

Three-Eyed and One-Eyed, hearing this, immediately

ONE-EYED, TWO-EYED, THREE-EYED   69

got to work. They jumped and stretched and strained, but whatever they did, they could not reach the uncooperative[67] branches of the tree.

'I simply don't know what's the matter!' said the old woman, laughing fakely[68]. 'They are usually so strong and flexible[69].'

'How funny,' said the suitor, faintly bored. No, he could not marry these ridiculous girls. He wanted a woman who was his equal.

Two-Eyed had been watching the entire scene from under the bed and was growing more and more frustrated. She had to do something, or she would be serving her wicked mother and idle[70] sisters for the rest of her miserable life. She still had the golden apple *she* had picked, so she threw it out from under the bed. Her throw was true[71], and the apple rolled along the ground and bumped into the man's shoe.

'Oh!' he said, picking it up and dusting it off[72]. '*Here* is one of the apples, but where on earth did it come from...?'

'I haven't the foggiest[73]!' said the mother, grabbing the apple out of his hand. 'Three-Eyed must have picked it earlier.'

Three-Eyed smiled eagerly at the man, but he ignored her, looking for the source of the apple. And there, shining from under the bed, he saw two bright eyes.

'Ah,' he said, pulling Two-Eyed out, 'your daughter has not run away at all!'

Two-Eyed blushed profusely[74], and could not look the

man in the eyes. He raised a finger to her chin and turned her head up to face him.

He was gorgeous from this distance, and his eyes shone like the golden apples.

'Your mother says that you do not want to get married. Is this true?'

'No, no, not at all!' said Two-Eyed. 'I would love nothing more than to marry you. That is, if you are—'

But before she could finish her sentence, the man kissed her.

'Yes,' he said softly.

Behind the two lovers, the rest of the family was having a meltdown[75]. Three-Eyed was weeping and sobbing, the mother was yanking out[76] her hair, and One-Eyed was still desperately trying to pick an apple.

'You cannot leave!' said the mother, as Two-Eyed linked hands with the suitor and left the house.

But the couple ignored her, and passed by the apple tree.

'I suppose you want me to pick you an apple?' said Two-Eyed. 'To prove I am a hard-working girl.'

'Oh no, not at all,' he said. 'That's what my father's always saying, that I must find a wife who can toil away in the midday sun. But I don't think that's important. I had a strange dream, you know, a few nights ago. A goatherd came and told me that I must marry the girl whose eyes glisten[77] like pure gold, and I believe I have found her.'

Two-Eyed was so overcome with emotion[78] that she

did not know how to respond. Instead, she just kissed him.

So they went and got married, and lived happily ever after. And the mother and her two favourite daughters never, ever in their long, miserable lives, could pick an apple from the tree.

THE BOY WHO KNEW NO FEAR

Once, there was a father with two sons, who he loved and loathed[1] in turn. The older son, Hugh, was smart, sensible and capable, while the younger son, Anders, was an idle[2] good-for-nothing[3]. Whenever the father needed help, Hugh was always quick to assist him, while Anders sat around idly.

But when he asked Hugh to go somewhere late at night, the boy turned pale and cried, 'Oh no, Father, I can't go out in the night! It makes me shudder[4] so.' And when his father told ghost stories by the fire, Hugh often said, 'Oh, it makes me shudder!'

Anders could not understand what his brother was talking about. There was nothing strange about the night. It was a lovely time, when the moon shone beautifully and the town was quiet. And he could not understand what Hugh's problem with Father's ghost stories was, either, since he always told them so well.

'He is always saying, "It makes me shudder, it makes me shudder!" It does not make *me* shudder, although I don't know what that means.'

One day, the father said to Anders, 'Alright, you worthless boy. Despite the empty space between your ears, you have grown tall and strong. You might just be able to make a decent living, but you'll need to learn a trade of some sort. Your brother studied woodwork[5], which you are almost certainly too stupid for, but we might find something that suits your particular lack of intelligence. What do you think?'

'Actually, Father,' he said, smirking[6], 'I know exactly what I want to learn. I want to learn how to *shudder*. I simply don't understand it.'

Hugh, who was eavesdropping[7] through the door, slapped his head and said, 'God, if only I had a donkey for a brother. Then he'd at least have *some* brains.'

'You want to learn how to *shudder*?' said Anders' father. 'I can teach you how to shudder right this instant, you stupid boy. Just get my belt and bend over.'

'Oh, you really will?' said Anders excitedly. 'Then please!'

He ran to get his father's belt, but his father shouted, 'Stop! It was a joke, you idiot.' As much as he wanted to shut Anders up, he wanted him to leave his home more. Perhaps if he agreed to his strange request, he could get rid of the boy forever.

A few days later, the perfect opportunity arose, when a

priest came to visit the house. The father invited him for a cup of tea and told him at length[8] about his son.

Hearing this, the priest lit up[9] and said, 'Ah, you truly have a special child. The Lord[10] sends us these children to test us, and I am confident I can help him. Let him live with me, and I will teach him how to shudder.

The father promptly agreed, and sent Anders on his way.

The priest lived in a house next to the church, and taught Anders about bell ringing. There was a great bell in the tower, and every day, Anders climbed up to ring it. A few days into Anders' education, the priest decided it was time he learned how to shudder. He woke Anders up in the middle of the night and told him to go ring the bell. While Anders was getting ready, the priest sneaked[11] up there before him.

The boy was letting out a fat yawn, and was just about to ring the bell, when he heard a noise behind him. He turned around and saw a man dressed in white bedsheets[12], standing at the top of the stairs.

'Who's that?' said Anders wearily[13].

But the man in white did not reply. He simply stood there, and started making strange sounds with his mouth, like he was sipping tea. Anders supposed he looked a bit like a ghost, although he didn't know which ghosts made such strange noises.

'Answer me,' said Anders, 'or leave. You have no business here.'

The priest waved his hands up and down, and made

THE BOY WHO KNEW NO FEAR   75

louder noises, trying to scare Anders. The boy just blinked at him, unsure what this strange man was up to[14].

'Look, I have a bell to be ringing and I don't want to stay up here all night. Say something, man, or I'll throw you down the stairs!'

He doesn't really mean that, thought the priest. *He's very good at hiding his fear, but I can see it growing, the way his face is turning red.*

But Anders was, in fact, just getting impatient. After all, why would he be scared of a man wearing bedsheets? The man continued to make strange noises and wave his arms, and Anders had had enough. He ran and pushed him down the stairs.

The 'ghost' screamed and fell ten steps backwards, landing painfully on the floor.

'That'll teach you[15] to wear weird clothes and pester[16] strangers in the night,' he said.

Then he rang the bell, stepped carefully over the 'ghost', and went to bed.

The priest's wife, meanwhile, was waiting for her husband to come back. He was gone for a very long time, and she started to worry, so she went and woke Anders.

'What is it now?!' he said. 'Does "shuddering" mean to be constantly woken up in the night?'

'Have you seen my husband? He went up to the tower before you.'

'Funny. No, I didn't see him. There was just a strange man dressed in white, making odd noises, and since he refused to answer my questions, I pushed him down the stairs.'

Horrified[17], the wife ran up to the tower and found her husband whimpering[18] in pain. He had broken his leg.

The next day, she went straight to Anders' father and shouted at him.

'Your boy has caused us no end of problems! He threw my husband down the stairs and broke his leg. We don't want him anymore.'

The father pulled Anders out of the house by his ear and said, 'What did you do, you stupid boy?!'

'Father,' said Anders, 'I did nothing wrong. That man is a pervert[19] of some kind. He followed me into the tower at night, dressed in white bedsheets, and stood there making strange noises. He wouldn't answer my questions, so I pushed him down the stairs. Aren't you proud of me?'

His father turned completely white.

'Ah yes, he looked a bit like that!'

'I have nothing to say to you, boy. Leave, and never come back.'

Anders shrugged[20]. 'If you say so. I agree. I think I can learn to shudder just fine by myself.'

The boy headed for the door, and the father hesitated. As much as he loathed[21] his stupid son, he still loved him as a father. So he said, 'Wait! I will not let you wander out to a cold death just like that. Take this money, but do not tell anyone who your father is.'

Anders smiled. 'Thanks, Dad!'

Anders walked out of town and through a forest, saying the whole time, 'If only I could shudder!'

Hanging is an old way to kill people. People were hanged on ropes like this.

A few hours later, he walked past a tree where seven men were hanged. Anders stared up at the tree and scratched his head. What on earth were they doing up there? It looked very uncomfortable.

It just so happened that there was another traveller going along that road at the same time, a conman[22]. He saw Anders staring up at the tree and thought, *That boy looks particularly stupid, and there's nobody easier to con than stupid boys. I think I'll have some fun with him.*

He strolled up to Anders and said, 'Greetings, fellow traveller! Where are you headed?'

'I'm off to learn how to shudder,' said Anders smugly[23]. It was such an exciting thing to learn, since he had no idea what it was.

The conman laughed. This was going to be a *very* easy con.

'Well, then you're in luck! I'm just the right man to teach you how to shudder, and I'll do it out of the goodness of my own heart[24].'

'Oh no, sir!' said Anders. 'I couldn't expect such a thing for free. What luck! I've been barely a day out of home and I'm already learning how to shudder! No, if you teach me, I'll give you *all* my money.'

The conman licked his lips. 'Alright, then! Take a look

up at that tree there.' He pointed at the place where the seven men were hanged. 'Those seven men wanted to marry the baker's daughter, and as you can imagine, the baker wanted to make sure they were suitable for her. So he told them that the man who can fly will take his daughter as a wife, and there they are, learning how to fly.'

'Wow!' said Anders. 'I want to join them.'

He started climbing the tree, but the conman grabbed his arm.

'Not quite yet! You wouldn't want to learn how to fly before you've learned how to shudder, would you?'

Anders thought for a moment. 'I suppose not. Can I do both at once?'

'Oh, my dear boy, by the time I've taught you you'll be flying, shuddering and dancing all at once! But one thing at a time. Sit by the tree and wait for the night, and whatever you do, *don't* fall asleep. By the morning, you will have learned how to shudder, I can guarantee[25] you.'

'Oh, you're going to write me a guarantee?' said Anders. 'Do you have paper and a pen in your cloak[26]?'

'It's a figure of speech[27],' said the conman, losing his patience. By God, this boy was an *idiot*. 'Anyway, sweet dreams! I'll see you tomorrow.'

'But you said not to sleep!' cried Anders as the man left.

Honestly, some people were terrible at giving instructions. But he did as the man said and sat by the tree.

As the night drew in[28], it got cold, so Anders made a

THE BOY WHO KNEW NO FEAR

fire. Then a sharp wind blew, and the hanged men swayed[29] in the wind.

Of course, the conman had expected that Anders would figure out that they were *not* learning to fly, and find the swaying men very frightening. But he had underestimated just how oblivious[30] Anders really was.

'You must be cold up there!' he called.

The men did not answer.

'Hello? How is it going? Getting close to flying?'

Again, the men did not answer. How rude! But they really did look cold, so Anders decided to help them. He climbed up the tree and cut them down. They fell onto the ground with a PLOP and he put them by the fire to warm up. But they didn't just warm up—the flames set their clothes on fire[31], and the men did nothing to stop it!

'Wow, you really are quite stupid!' said Anders. 'Aren't you going to move away? Or is this part of learning how to fly?'

The dead men did not reply, and their clothes continued to burn. This made Anders quite angry.

'No teacher worth their salt[32] would make you burn your own clothes like that! I can't stand watching you waste precious fabric. Your mothers must have sewn for hours to make those!'

So Anders huffily[33] hanged them back on the tree, and then went and slept by the fire. He knew that he wasn't supposed to sleep, but he couldn't see how he was going to learn to shudder from these foolish men, and besides, he wasn't particularly fond of teachers at the moment.

The next day, the conman found him shivering in the morning light.

'Well, did you learn how to shudder?'

'No!' said Anders, leaping to his feet[34]. 'Those men were so stupid! They wouldn't answer my questions, which I was taught is rude, and then they let their clothes burn as if their mothers hadn't worked hard to make them. How could I learn to shudder from such foolish, selfish people?'

The conman couldn't believe his ears. In fact, he was so dismayed[35] that he shuddered. But before he could ask for his payment, the boy was already leaving.

'Wait!' he called. 'What about my money?'

'I learned nothing from you!' shouted Anders. 'Go shudder yourself, whatever that means!'

So the boy continued out of the forest and passed through a village, always saying, 'If only I could shudder!'

A man from the village saw him and thought, *That boy looks lost. I should help him.*

He stopped him and asked, 'What are you called, boy?'

Anders thought for a moment. 'Well, my father always calls me "stupid".'

'And where are you from?'

'A house. Isn't everyone?'

The villager sighed. This wasn't going to be easy.

'Who is your father?'

Anders' face suddenly turned serious. 'I cannot tell you.'

'And what is it you were saying to yourself, just now?'

'I said, "If only I could shudder!" You see, I want to learn to shudder.'

The man frowned[36]. 'Why on earth would you want to learn that? Well, I know a way you can learn, but it won't be pleasant.'

'Oh, please, sir! I'll do *anything* to learn how to shudder. How much should I pay you?'

The man licked his lips. He'd wanted to help the boy, but it appeared that this boy was beyond help. And didn't he deserve some compensation[37] for being such a good citizen and helping people like this?

'I'll gladly accept whatever money you have to offer. Uh, maybe more than that. Yes, that's perfect. Well then, you've likely heard of the King, but many don't know that he lived in a different castle before. Now it stands empty, and only ghosts and monsters inhabit[38] it. The King is seeking a man brave enough to stay in the castle for three nights. Whoever does so will be given his daughter's hand in marriage[39], and let me tell you, she is the most beautiful woman to ever exist.'

He left out the part about her personality. The only reason the King needed her future husband to stay in the haunted castle was to prove he could handle the Princess's cruel ways. She was famous for playing tricks on people.

'I get to learn how to shudder *and* marry a princess? Jackpot[40]!'

'There is more. There are also fantastic treasures in the castle, guarded by the monsters. If you succeed, you will gain the treasures and the girl, and you will live in comfort for the rest of your life.'

'How wonderful!' said Anders. He couldn't understand why nobody had completed the trial already. Ghosts and monsters were a bit odd, but they were quite fun, too.

The villager, seeing that Anders didn't understand the danger, suddenly felt responsible. He couldn't let the boy just walk into his death without knowing what he was doing.

'Many men have gone into the castle, but none have left,' he said mysteriously.

Hmm, thought Anders. *Perhaps it is simply a very comfortable castle and they saw no reason to leave.*

So Anders went and told the King he would do the trial.

'You're very brave, my boy,' said the King, looking at him as if he thought he was actually very stupid. 'You may take three things with you into the castle.'

'Wow, this just gets easier and easier! In that case… I would like a fire, a knife and a lathe[41].'

He hated sleeping in the cold, so a fire was essential. Knives were always useful, too. And he'd seen his brother playing with his lathe, when he did woodwork[42]. Anders had always wanted to try it, but his brother never let him. Something about Anders breaking it.

'A lathe? Are you sure? Don't you want something more useful? Maybe an axe? What can a lathe do?'

'A lathe can do lots of things!' said Anders. 'At least, my brother does lots with it.'

'Fine, fine. But do be careful, my boy.'

Anders shrugged[43]. 'It's just a haunted castle. What could go wrong?'

So Anders went to the castle, which was lying in ruins. Anders had never seen ruins before, so he thought, *Wow, what a strange architectural decision. It looks interesting, but it's so cold with all those holes in the ceiling!*

An axe (pronunciation AKS). People use axes to cut wood.

He found a nice room with a chair in it, so he made a fire and sat down by the lathe.

'If only I could shudder!' he said. 'Somehow, I don't think I'm going to learn it here.'

Just then, he heard a cry from a dark corner.

'Ow, meow! It is so cold!'

'If you are cold, come and sit by the fire, silly!'

When you curl up, you move into this shape.

Two great black cats jumped out of the darkness and sat beside him. Their eyes shone like hot coals. They curled up by the fire, warming themselves nicely, before saying, 'Ow, meow! Shall we play a game of cards?'

Anders didn't like the look of these cats. Black cats knew magic, his mother always told him. So he said, 'Yes, let's. But first, I wonder, do black cats have black paws? Or do you have pink paws like other cats?'

'Ow, meow! Mind your business[44], boy.' They

suddenly seemed very reluctant, and moved back into the darkness.

Anders raised an eyebrow. 'Well, if you won't show me your paws, then I won't play your games.'

So the cats did so, raising their paws up to show that they were pink, and they had *very* sharp claws.

'Oh, what long claws you have! Let me cut them for you. I have a knife.'

A paw (animal hand) with long claws (they can hurt you!)

'No!' said the cats, snatching their paws away[45]. 'We need them to hold onto the cards.'

Anders shook his head. 'But you'll just scratch them! I can't play cards if they're all covered in scratches. It's simply not decent. Please, let me cut your claws.'

'Fine,' said the cats.

They came close, and Anders saw his opportunity. He grabbed the cats by the throat and held the knife up at them. 'I know what you want, you monsters! You want to claw my eyes out, or cast some magic spell[46] on me! Well no, thank you!'

And with that, he threw the cats out of the window. They meowed and screamed as they fell into the water below. But before Anders could sit down again, hundreds of black cats and black dogs swarmed[47] out of the darkness. Their eyes all shone like hot coals, and they shouted and bit at him, and tried to put out the fire.

'Get back, you beasts[48]!' he shouted.

THE BOY WHO KNEW NO FEAR

He waved his knife around, and some of the animals cried and ran away. Others stayed and fought, and those ones he grabbed by the ears and threw them out the window. But the animals kept coming and coming, filling the room, pushing him to the floor. He was losing hope, but at the stroke of midnight[49], all the creatures suddenly disappeared.

When Anders sat down again, he felt very tired. He turned around and saw a bed in the corner.

'Perfect!' he said, and climbed into the bed.

But as he fell asleep, the bed started moving. He opened his eyes, and saw that the bed was crawling[50] around the room like a bug.

'Wonderful,' he said. 'That will help lull[51] me to sleep. But go a bit faster, would you?'

So the bed ran and ran, moving around the castle like a horse, and Anders made himself very comfortable. The bed then flipped over[52], so that it was lying on top of him.

'That's no fun,' he said. 'I told you I wanted you to *lull* me to sleep.' He pushed the bed off him and went to sleep by the fire.

In the morning, the King came and saw him lying still on the floor.

'Oh no, the poor boy! The ghosts and monsters must have killed him.'

'What are you talking about?' said Anders, yawning and sitting up.

'You're alive! What happened?'

'Good morning to you, too! Many things happened

last night, but the important thing is, I did *not* learn how to shudder. Still, it was a very lively evening anyway.'

'You mean, you were not afraid?'

'Of course not! I slept very well.'

So the next night Anders went back into the haunted castle and said again, 'If only I could shudder!'

This time, there were no cats or dogs, but a few hours later, he heard a loud scream, and something fell from the chimney. It was a man, but only the top half of him. He was missing his legs and feet, and blood was pouring out of his torso[53].

'Hello!' cried Anders. 'That must be quite uncomfortable. Where's the rest of your body?'

Then there was another scream, and the other half of the man fell down.

'Let me make a fire for you,' he said, thinking that the man might be cold.

When he turned around, the two halves had stitched themselves back together[54], and the man was sitting on the chair with an evil smile on his face.

'Excuse me, that chair is mine.'

Anders pushed him onto the floor.

The man growled[55] and jumped to his feet. 'We'll see whose chair it is! Let us play a game.'

He clapped his hands, and some leg bones fell from the chimney, complete with human feet on the ends.

'Ooh, we're going to go bowling!' said Anders. 'I love this game.' He placed the leg bones in a triangle and then looked around. 'But uh, where is the ball?'

The evil man rolled his eyes[56] and clapped his hands again. This time, some skulls fell down.

'These are terrible balls! They're not round at all.'

'They'll be more than good enough—'

'No!' said Anders. 'If we're going to play, we're going to do it right.'

So he took the skulls and put them on the lathe, working them until they were round.

Bowling (pronunciation BO-ling)

'There! Now they'll roll perfectly.'

They went bowling, and Anders did quite badly, but he had a lot of fun. The man wanted to scare him, but Anders was completely oblivious[57], and wondered why the man kept saying, 'Boo!' Once more, at the stroke of midnight[58], everything disappeared: the man, the skulls and the leg bones.

A skull

'Oh no! I did not get to say goodbye.'

With nothing else to do, Anders lay down and went to sleep.

The next morning, the King came and spoke to him again.

'How was it this time?'

'Quite fun! We went bowling, although my friend did not say goodbye.'

'But you did not learn how to shudder?'

'No! I'm starting to think I'll *never* learn…'

On the third night, Anders sat sadly on his chair and said, 'If only I could shudder!'

A few hours later, six tall men with pale white faces entered the room with a coffin[59], which they placed on the ground before Anders.

Hmm, thought Anders. *Why would they be bringing me a coffin?*

Then he remembered that, a few days before his father had kicked him out, his cousin had passed away. Perhaps they were bringing him his body so he could say goodbye?

The pale men opened the coffin, but the man inside was too big to be Anders' cousin. Still, the boy was convinced that it was him, and said, 'Cousin! You look so cold. Let me warm you up.'

So he warmed his hand on the fire and held it to the man's face. But the body stayed cold. Anders carried him out of the coffin and put him by the fire, but this didn't help either. Finally, Anders put him in the bed and wrapped him in the bedsheets.

Eventually, the body warmed up, and started to move.

'See, cousin? You must feel much better, now that you are warm. I never understood why dead people have to sleep in coffins, anyway. It must be so cold under the ground.'

The dead man sat up and cried, 'Foolish boy! Now I will devour[60] you!'

'What?!' said Anders. 'That's how you thank me, by

trying to eat me? You always were my least favourite cousin. Back to the coffin!'

He picked up his 'cousin' like he was made of feathers, threw him back into the coffin and shut the lid. The six pale men came back, rolled their eyes[61] at Anders, and took the coffin away.

'Don't you want to stay for a round of bowling[62]? Ugh, fine. I'm sick of this place. I don't think I will *ever* learn to shudder!'

'I can help you with that…'

Anders turned around and saw an old man with a long white beard, leering[63] from the darkness.

'You will shudder the whole time while I strangle[64] you!'

'Strangle me? That doesn't sound very fun!'

'Too bad! I'm going to kill you!'

The man jumped at Anders, but the boy pushed him to the ground.

'I don't think so. You're not very strong.'

'Oh, I might not *look* strong, but I am,' said the old man, standing up. 'Fine then, let's have a little competition, a test of strength. Follow me…'

The man guided Anders through many dark passages, revealing parts of the castle Anders had never seen before. Finally, they arrived in a room with two big stones and an axe.

'It's very simple. We shall each try to split the stone to see who is stronger.'

The old man grabbed the axe, wielding[65] it with

surprising strength. His beard dangled[66] as he moved. He swung the axe, breaking the stone cleanly in two with it.

Anders was worried. He didn't think he was strong enough to break his stone, and he really didn't want to be strangled. But he wasn't scared. He had a plan.

'Pah! I can do better than that.'

He took the axe and held it above the second stone. The old man stood and watched. Anders waited and waited, wielding the axe but not moving. The old man moved closer and closer, his beard dangling in front of him. When he was close enough, Anders dropped the axe, grabbed the man's beard, and pulled it between the two broken pieces of stone. Then he pushed the stone together, trapping his beard inside.

'Hey, hey!' cried the old man. 'I can't move! That's cheating!'

'Now I have you,' said Anders. 'You were going to strangle me, you nasty old thing!'

Then he took a piece of stone and beat the old man with it until he was black and blue[67].

'Please stop!' he cried. 'I'm sorry I threatened to strangle you! I'll show you where the treasures are hidden!'

Anders' arm got tired, so he stopped. He had completely forgotten about the treasures and the Princess, but he supposed that it would be nice to have them. Even if he didn't learn to shudder here, he would have something.

'Fine, then.'

He released the old man, who showed him a hidden door in the wall, which led to a room with three huge chests[68] full of treasure.

'One of these chests is for the poor, one is for the King, and the other is yours.'

'Oh, so the monsters like giving to the poor, do they?'

But just at that moment, it turned midnight, and the old man disappeared. All the candles in the room went out, leaving Anders in the darkness. He carefully found his way back to the fire and slept there.

The next morning, the King came and said, 'Surely now you have learnt what shuddering is?'

'No, I have not. My dead cousin visited, and then a bearded[69] man came and showed me where the treasure is, but *nobody* taught me to shudder.'

The King gasped[70]. 'Then you have completed the trial, and you can marry my daughter!'

'Yes, yes, hooray[71] for Anders, hooray for the poor. But I don't care about all that! I still don't know how to shudder!'

The King ignored him, and made him show him to the treasures. They carried out the three chests, gave one to the poor, one to the King, and one to Anders. Then they held a great wedding, and Anders finally met his bride.

Just as the legends said, she was indeed a cruel, unusual woman. She played all kinds of tricks on Anders, so he started playing tricks on her, too, which she loved. They had lots of fun together, and she never once called him stupid, so he fell quite in love with her.

But still, Anders could not be fully happy. Every night, when he went to bed, he sighed and said, 'If only I could shudder!'

Finally, this got to be too much for his wife. 'Fine then, I will really show him how to shudder!'

She woke up early in the morning and went out to the river. She filled a bucket with cold water and fish and carried it inside. Then she poured the bucket right over Anders' head!

Anders sat up and cried, 'Oh, what makes me shudder so much? What makes me shudder so, my wife? Ah! Finally I know how to shudder!'

And they lived happily ever after.

CINDERELLA

Once upon a time, there was a poor girl called Cinderella. Her mother had died when she was young, and her father married another woman. Cinderella's stepmother was a horrible person, and had two daughters herself: Freta and Greta.

Freta and Greta treated Cinderella like dirt, making her do all the cooking, cleaning and sewing, and when their father tried to suggest that *they* do some work, their mother always said, 'Don't be so cruel!' So Cinderella lived a life of misery, doing all the work in the house, wearing ugly, torn clothes and sleeping in the dust and ashes[1] in the fireplace.

The only nice thing in Cinderella's life was the hazel tree in the garden. Her mother had asked her to plant it over her grave when she died, and every night Cinderella sat by the tree and cried. It was big and strong, and sometimes when she sat against the tree, she felt like her mother was holding her, if only for a second. She was also great friends with two little birds who lived in the tree, and whenever her stepsisters weren't looking, she liked to play with them and sing songs.

Hazel trees make hazelnuts, that look like this.

One day, while Cinderella was sweeping the kitchen under the punishing eyes of her stepsisters, her stepmother came in to make an announcement.

'The King has announced a ball[2] and all are invited,' she said, holding out a letter.

Freta and Greta cheered, laughed and clapped, until their mother held out her hand to silence them.

'It will be three days long—'

More cries of joy.

'—and there, the Prince will choose his new wife.'

The two sisters gasped[3], and practically fainted, already dreaming about dancing with the handsome prince and becoming his wife.

Cinderella had never been to a ball before, but she had always wanted to go to one. And this was in the palace! Oh, what wonderful people would be there, what beautiful clothes, what delicious food... She didn't care much about the Prince, because she had never met him, but she desperately wished to go to the ball.

Over the next few days, the family launched into mad preparations. Greta and Freta went into town with their mother to buy dresses, which Cinderella then had to tailor[4] to fit them. Every day, they asked her to fashion[5] new bows, try out new hairstyles and modify their dresses, but the next day they always changed their mind and asked her to do something else.

A bow (pronunciation BO)

In a quiet moment, of which there were few, Cinderella went to her father and asked him if she could go to the ball. He was keeping well away from the whole affair, but when she asked, he smiled.

'I don't see why not!'

Cinderella took this to mean that she could go, and over the next few days she did her best to make some decent clothes for herself, making sure to hide her work from her stepsisters.

But on the day of the ball, when Cinderella put on her dress and announced she was ready to go, Freta and Greta simply laughed in her face.

'You want to go to the King's ball in *that?!* That dress looks like it was made by rats! It's not worthy of even a walk down the road[6].'

'But Father said—'

'Cinderella!' cried her stepmother. 'Do you really think we would allow you to go to the ball and embarrass[7] us? If you were invited, I would have told you.'

'Don't worry, Cindy!' said Freta. 'You'll have something to distract you.'

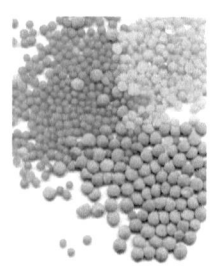
Different types of lentils

'Here you go!' said Greta, handing her a pot filled with lentils. 'While we're gone, pick out the bad lentils from the good ones.'

'If there's even *one* bad lentil in there when we come back, you'll have to start all over again!'

Holding back tears[8], Cinderella watched the rest of her family climb into their carriage[9] and ride off to the palace.

Oh, how awful she felt! She poured all the lentils out on the floor, but it was clear that the work would take at least until midnight, and she didn't have the will to do it.

She ran outside and threw herself onto the ground next to her mother's tree, sobbing into the earth.

A minute later, she heard a bird singing by her ear, and looked up to see her two bird friends.

'What's wrong, Cinderella?' said one of them.

'You can talk?'

'Of course, of course. What's wrong, Cinderella?'

'Oh, it's only that… I was an idiot, really. I thought I could go to the King's ball, but of course I can't. I have to separate lentils in the dust while my sisters dance with wonderful people.'

'Show us these lentils, show us.'

So Cinderella took the birds inside and showed them the pile of lentils.

'We can help, we can help! We will eat the bad and leave the good.'

'Oh, I appreciate it. But I still cannot go to the ball!'

'Cinderella, Cinderella. Go out to the tree and shake it.'

The birds started working, and Cinderella walked sadly to the tree. She did not know why they were asking her to shake the tree, but she did as she was told.

Out of the tree fell a large hazelnut. She opened the shell, but inside there was not a nut, but a beautiful green gown[10]! It was as beautiful as a fresh flower in spring.

Cautiously, Cinderella shook the tree again, and another nut fell out. This time, there was not a dress inside, but a pair of gorgeous green shoes!

Her heart beating in her chest, she tried on the dress and shoes, and they fit her perfectly.

'Oh, Mother, thank you! But how shall I go to the ball without a carriage?'

She shook the tree once more, and yet another nut fell[11]. When she opened this one, a beautiful carriage with two horses and a servant jumped out.

'Wow!' she said. 'I must go and get ready!'

Cinderella ran inside, washed herself, combed her hair and put on her clothes. She was unrecognisable without the usual dirt and torn clothes. She was beautiful.

The birds had finished with the lentils, and they flew around her happily, singing, 'To the ball, to the ball! But be careful, my dear. You must return before midnight, or all will be lost.'

Cinderella climbed into the carriage and rode to the ball. She could hardly believe it was happening, and when she arrived at the palace, she had to pinch¹² herself to make sure she wasn't dreaming.

Everything was just as she had imagined it, and more. The building was made of beautiful white stone, with a long marble staircase leading to the entrance, and inside it was filled with magnificent coloured lights, flowers from all around the world and the most distinguished guests with the most wonderful dresses.

Marble, a type of stone

Cinderella felt at once uncomfortable. She didn't belong there. Her dress was so simple compared to everyone else, and she didn't know how to dance.

For a while, she merely watched the dances, but not long after, a man came and spoke to her.

'May I dance with you?'

He was the most handsome man she'd ever met, with hair as black as the night and eyes that shone like stars.

'Yes, of course,' she said, taking his hand.

As the two danced, she felt all eyes turn to her. He was handsome, but to attract such attention? Whispers spread around the room, and as her dance partner spun her she heard bits of conversations: '...beautiful girl...' '...who is she?...' '...and with the Prince!'

Cinderella went as red as a tomato. She was dancing with the Prince himself!

The Prince smiled at her, saying, 'You dance well for someone who's never done it before.'

'How did you know?'

'It's obvious, but don't worry. I like it.'

They continued to spin around, and Cinderella caught a glimpse of her sisters, standing in the corner. Freta and Greta were making faces like frogs that had just been stood on, pulling at their dresses in rage.

Cinderella smiled and let herself enjoy the dance. By the time the song ended, she felt truly free, that was, until she heard the clock strike eleven[13].

Suddenly she remembered what the birds had said: return before midnight or all will be lost.

'I must go,' Cinderella said, moving out of the Prince's grip.

'Wait! Please stay for another dance.'

'Perhaps tomorrow night,' she said, before hurrying out the door.

She felt the Prince's stare on her back as she went. She ran down the marble staircase into her carriage and rode home.

Her heart beat madly the whole way. Never in her life had she experienced such joy. She wondered if her sisters had seen her, and hoped desperately that they were too stupid to put two and two together[14].

When she arrived home, she quickly hid the dress and shoes in the tree in the garden, changed into her normal clothes, messed up her hair and rubbed dust and dirt on her face.

When the others returned a few hours later, Cinderella heard Freta loudly declare, 'I hope Cinderella hasn't fallen asleep while sorting those lentils!'

'Forget the lentils,' said Greta. 'Just who was that strange girl?'

Cinderella breathed a sigh of relief. Her family came in to see her, and she put on a miserable expression, as if she'd spent the whole evening sorting lentils on the floor.

'Done already?' said Freta, sounding disappointed. 'We shall have to give you something more challenging tomorrow night.'

Greta yawned. 'Come on, Sister, let's go to bed.'

Cinderella smiled and said, 'Good night!'

Her stepmother stared at her suspiciously. 'Your hair looks different.'

'Oh?' Cinderella said, adjusting it self-consciously. 'I tied it up while I worked.'

'Hrmm. Do not get any strange ideas in your head about going to the ball tomorrow night or the next. You will stay here and work, understand?'

'Yes, Stepmother.'

'That's "Mother", you ungrateful little...!' She raised her hand to hit Cinderella, who covered her head and shut her eyes. But her stepmother took a deep breath and held back her anger. 'Good night, Cinderella.'

There was no doubt about it. She knew something was up[15].

Cinderella hardly slept that night, playing the ball over and over in her head. Oh, how handsome the Prince had been!

The next day, her sisters gave her double the chores to

work on, but she worked with great vigour[16], cleaning everything up in no time.

'Why are you smiling so much, Cinderella?' said Greta. 'You're not going to the ball, you know!'

'Oh, I know! I just had a lovely dream.'

'Well, dream on!' said Freta.

Part of Cinderella's joy came from overhearing[17] her sisters' conversation. Evidently, her dance with the Prince had been on *everyone's* lips, and it was deeply satisfying to hear how bothered they were by her presence at the ball. If only they knew!

That night, Freta and Greta dumped[18] a huge sack of seeds into Cinderella's hands. Then, deciding that was too nice, they knocked it on the floor.

'Pick out the good seeds, lazybones[19],' said Freta.

'And if we find even *one* bad one in there—'

'—you'll make me start again?'

Greta frowned[20]. 'Yeah. Now shut your mouth and get to work!'

Once the rest of the family had left, Cinderella's bird friends came in through the window.

'Oh, I know it is a lot to ask, but... would you help me again tonight?'

'Of course, Cinderella, of course!' sang the birds. 'Go and shake the tree, shake shake shake.'

So Cinderella ran out to the garden and shook the hazel tree once more. She was worried that the beautiful gifts might not fall down, but thankfully, they did.

This time, she had a gorgeous blue gown, blue as the

sea, with a pair of long gloves and dancing shoes. The shoes had a small heel, but after trying them on, Cinderella found she could walk just fine, and she felt beautiful in them.

'Goodbye, little birds!' she said, running out to the carriage, 'and thank you once more!'

'Remember, remember, return before midnight!'

This time, when Cinderella arrived everyone was waiting for her. There were gasps[21] as she entered the room, as they clearly had not been expecting her to be even more beautiful than the night before. Several men immediately came up to ask for a dance, but she refused them all, as there was only one she was interested in.

'I must admit,' said the Prince as they started to dance, 'I was worried you wouldn't return after your quick exit last night.'

'I apologise for my rudeness.'

'Are you going to tell me why you left? A man must wonder...'

'I assure you, it was through no fault of your own. I had... a matter to attend to[22].'

'Well, you are just as mysterious as you are beautiful. Will you at least give me the pleasure of knowing where you are from?'

'I come from not far from here.'

'And yet I have never heard of you until this moment! Won't you at least tell me your name?'

'I am Bridget.'

That was Cinderella's true name, that her mother had

chosen before she died. She was sure that her sisters would not remember it, having used her nickname for so long.

'A beautiful name.'

This time, Cinderella danced until past eleven, but as the time moved nearer to midnight, she kept looking at the clock.

'Other matters to attend to tonight as well?'

'Yes, I am afraid, my Prince.'

'Well, will I have the pleasure of seeing you again tomorrow night?'

'Absolutely.'

'Then I suppose I can let you go,' he said, smiling.

So Cinderella left once more, running down the steps and into the carriage before anyone else could question her.

Once again, after arriving home she hid the dress and shoes, dirtied herself and acted as if she had been working all evening. She made sure to mess up her hair just the way it had been before.

'Oh, I'll kill that girl!' said Greta, as they walked through the door.

'Some were saying she is a foreign princess,' said Freta. 'Pah! I think she looked *horrible* in that dress.'

'Girls, go to bed,' said their mother sternly[23]. 'No staying up late talking, understood?'

'Yes, mother!' they cried.

They stuck their heads into the room where Cinderella was and stuck out their tongues at her.

'We're going to give you *even more* work tomorrow, Cindy!'

Then they climbed up the stairs, laughing and chatting about the handsome men they'd met.

Cinderella was ready to sleep as well, but once again her stepmother came in to see her.

'Cinderella, dear child.'

Cinderella felt an icy cold pass through her body. Her stepmother only called her 'dear child' when she wanted something.

'Yes, Mother?'

'Remind me what name you had previously.'

Cinderella panicked, and said, 'Britney.' She should have chosen something much more different to her real name, but it just slipped out of her mouth.

'Oh?' said her stepmother, arching an eyebrow[24]. 'I could have sworn[25] you were called Bridget.'

'To be honest, Mother, I am so accustomed to my new name that I can hardly remember my old one!'

'Hmm,' said her stepmother, unconvinced. 'Well, you have worked well again tonight. Do not disappoint me tomorrow.'

Cinderella slept badly that night. She was haunted by nightmares of her stepmother. She dreamt that she travelled to the ball for the final night, but as she danced, her stepmother came and ripped off her dress, revealing her awful rags[26] beneath.

'See? She is nothing but a common servant girl!'

Cinderella woke up feeling sick.

That day, her sisters gave her plenty of chores, as promised. She had to water the flowers, cut the grass and feed all the animals, as well as her usual cleaning. But as she worked, she overheard[27] her sisters talking.

'Oh, it is so rotten that we only have one more night! I am not sure we have had a real chance yet...'

'Don't worry, tonight is the night! We'll dance with *him* tonight, no matter what that ugly girl tries, and we'll get married.'

'Not "we", stupid! We can't share a prince! He's going to be *mine*.'

'No! He'll be mine!'

They started fighting, but their words troubled Cinderella. She had enjoyed the ball so much that she had hardly thought about the future. As lovely as the Prince was, she would never be with him forever, because at midnight the magic would end and all her fine clothes would disappear. She would be a dirty, common servant girl, and he would be the handsome Prince.

Still, that night she couldn't stop herself from getting excited. Even if it was only three nights, they would be the most wonderful three nights of her life, and she had no intention of wasting this one with worries of the future.

This time, her sisters gave her three giant sacks of peas to sort through.

'You'll be up all night with these!' said the girls as they headed out the door. 'If you don't see us again, it's because we're getting married to the Prince!'

Cinderella waved goodbye, forcing herself not to

smile. Then, once she was sure they were safely out of sight, she let the birds in.

'I feel so bad to burden[28] you with so much work...'

'Nonsense, nonsense! It's the last night, the last night. Go and enjoy yourself!'

So while the birds worked, she went and shook the tree. Tonight, the dress was ten times as beautiful as the one from the night before. It was a gorgeous long silver gown, covered in shining stones, with a pair of delicate high heels.

'Goodness, I don't know if I'll be able to walk in these...'

But as soon as she put them on, she found a powerful energy filled her. She walked with complete grace, every part an elegant princess.

'Oh, how wonderful tonight will be!' she said to herself as she left.

When she arrived at the palace, the whole party gasped as she walked in, and then applauded. She had outdone herself[29], and she heard more than one whisper about how elegant she looked.

For a moment, the Prince looked sad.

'What's wrong, my Prince?'

'I am simply amazed by your extraordinary beauty. I have never seen a dress or shoes quite like that... Come, let us dance!'

Cinderella danced with the Prince, and for the first time in many years she felt truly happy. She felt no worry, no sadness or pain, and when she saw her sisters she did not even feel bitterness towards them, although they certainly felt it towards her.

She enjoyed herself so much that she hardly noticed the time going by. Everything seemed to stand still when she stared into the Prince's eyes, which was where she looked the entire evening, as they maintained a silent conversation with their bodies.

After what felt like far too little time, the clock began to strike and Cinderella woke up from her dream. She looked desperately at the clock. It was twelve!

'I'm so sorry, my Prince, but I must leave.'

She moved out of his arms and ran through the hall. The clock struck behind her: two, three, four.

'Wait!' cried the Prince, grabbing her hand. 'You cannot leave. I must know—'

'You cannot!'

Five, six, seven.

Cinderella pulled herself free and ran outside, heading for the steps.

Eight, nine.

If you stand on glue, your feet will get stuck.

But the Prince had predicted that she might attempt a quick escape, so he covered the steps with glue, and as she ran down them her shoes got stuck.

Ten, eleven.

Desperate to get away before the spell was broken[30], she pulled her feet out of the shoes, leaving them stuck to the steps, and ran into the night.

Twelve.

As she ran, her beautiful dress began to disintegrate[31], melting back into the ugly rags she had worn before. Her hair lost its bounce[32], turning ragged and dirty, and her worn old working shoes returned to her feet.

Her carriage was nowhere to be seen, and fearing that the Prince would chase her, she ran all the way home, arriving sweating like a farm animal.

She burst through the door, threw herself on the floor and started sobbing. Oh, what a wonderful evening it had been, and how quickly it had gone! Now she had to return to her sad, painful existence, and she never even got to kiss the Prince.

Cinderella cried for several hours, before pulling herself together[33] and cleaning herself up. She couldn't let her awful sisters and stepmother see her tears, so she covered her face with dust to hide the redness in her cheeks.

The arrival of the rest of the family came with plenty of noise, Freta and Greta laughing cheerfully at some joke one of them had made.

'Shh!' said their stepmother. 'You'll wake up the neighbours.'

'Oh, but Mother, it was such a wonderful night! And I *do* believe that man wants to marry me.'

'That man has only a small fortune. You were supposed to seduce[34] the Prince.'

'But that's not fair! That awful foreign princess stole

him away the whole night. What were we supposed to do?'

'You were supposed to do better. Now off to bed.'

Thankfully, Freta and Greta did not pop in to talk to Cinderella, but her stepmother did.

She stood there in the door frame with a grave expression[35] on her face. Outlined in the moonlight, she looked like a dead person who had come back to life and climbed out of the earth.

'It was a lovely evening, wasn't it?'

'I wouldn't know, Mother, as I was working.'

Her stepmother smiled briefly. 'And you managed to sort all those peas very well. I would've said that was two nights' work.'

'I did not stop once.'

'How lucky we are to have you, Bridget.'

Cinderella was surprised to hear her name, and her stepmother smiled as she saw the look on Cinderella's face.

'Remember, my dear, you will always live here. There are no happy endings or handsome princes for you, understand?'

'Yes, Mother.'

'Good. Now get some sleep. From tomorrow, you will be helping Freta and Greta prepare for their weddings, as they are sure to be proposed to.'

Cinderella lay down in the fireplace and waited for her stepmother to leave. She felt sick. That was what the rest of her life would consist of: waiting on her horrible stepsisters hand and foot[36]. Even if they got married, she expected they'd bring her with them, splitting her up between the two of them to do all their work.

'Oh, Mother,' whispered Cinderella. 'If only you were here.'

The next morning, the whole family was awoken early by a trumpet playing in the street.

'All listen! There is a royal announcement!' cried a male voice. Cinderella ran to the window. It was one of the King's men, standing on a carriage and reading from a piece of paper. 'The King is searching for the future bride of his son, the Prince. She who can wear these shoes and walk as if on air shall be the Prince's bride.'

The man held up a pair of shoes—Cinderella's shoes from the night before! Somehow, the spell had not taken them. Cinderella's heart beat fast. If she could try them on…

'Me first!' shouted Greta, charging down the stairs.

'No, me!' cried Freta.

They started fighting, and ended up falling down into a pile on the floor.

'Girls!' commanded their mother. 'Get up at once and stop making a fool of yourselves! If you are going to be the Prince's bride then you must act royal.'

Cinderella watched in horror as they walked out to try on the shoes. But the King's servant simply held the shoes up to their feet and said, 'Sorry, ma'am, but these feet will never fit into the shoes.'

'Well, aren't you at least going to try?'

'Can't damage them before anyone else gets to try them, can we? I'll tell you what[37], if your daughters' feet magically shrink in the next few hours, they can try 'em on.'

Furious, the stepmother walked her daughters back inside and said, 'Freta, come with me into the kitchen.'

She took her into the room and shut the door behind her. Confused, Greta and Cinderella met eyes, but the girl just said, 'What are you looking at, Snotarella[38]?'

While the stepmother talked to Freta, Greta went to pick out a dress 'for her wedding.'

'I suppose there is no magnificent dress waiting in the tree for me today…' said Cinderella sadly.

With nothing else to do, she went and pressed her ear to the kitchen door to hear what her stepmother and stepsister were talking about.

'Mother, no!' came Freta's voice.

'Stop whining[39], child! It will only hurt for a bit, but you will have a lifetime of happiness afterwards. You can pay for new feet when you're queen.'

'Mother, I'm scared!'

Freta started crying, and then came some sounds of struggle between them, before the girl screamed so loudly it hurt Cinderella's ears.

'Be quiet!' shouted the stepmother.

Cinderella's eyes widened. She couldn't be, surely…?

Whatever horrible operation had been going on, it sounded like it was over, so Cinderella ran and hid in the corner. A few moments later, the door burst open, her mother carrying Freta in her arms.

The girl was forcing down tears, pale as a sheet, but what caught Cinderella's attention were her feet. They had bandages wrapped around them, and blood was already starting to show through.

The stepmother carried Freta outside to the King's servant, pushing past the other townspeople.

'My daughter's feet were a little swollen due to the cold weather. The shoes will fit perfectly now.'

Cinderella watched in horror through the window. The stepmother did a clever job of hiding the girl's feet until the shoes were on, and once they were, she pushed the girl forward.

'Walk, dear,' she whispered.

But Freta just fell forward like a baby duck, tripping up and landing in the man's arms.

'This is not the girl,' he said, pushing her back. 'The girl the Prince is looking for walks as if on air, not mud.'

Freta burst into tears, pulled off the shoes and ran upstairs. For the first time in her life, Cinderella felt genuinely sorry for her.

'Who's next?' called the man.

The stepmother stomped[40] inside and called Greta in to the kitchen, but after seeing what had happened to her sister, the girl had to be pulled kicking and screaming.

'It'll just hurt for a second, dear. Think of how rich we'll be afterwards!'

Cinderella covered her ears, but she still heard the

screams. Oh, how awful it was! Then, when it was over, she went and watched through the window as Greta went to try on the magic shoes.

Greta put on a brave face, and tried to walk gracefully, but it was clear how much pain she was in, and she only managed a few shaky steps before stopping.

'Better,' said the man, 'but hardly graceful. I think not.'

Greta bit her lip, forced a smile, and handed back the shoes.

'What's all this racket about[41]?' said Cinderella's father, coming down the stairs. 'I heard you screaming,' he said, looking questioningly at Greta.

'The Prince is looking for his bride, the mysterious princess,' she said. 'Whoever can walk in her shoes can marry him. But, but, but me and Freta failed!'

She started crying and fell into her father's arms.

'There, there, dear,' he said without much enthusiasm. 'Oh, Cinderella! Why don't you try?'

'Absolutely not!' cried her stepmother. 'She's a dirty servant girl and nothing more.'

'Excuse me?' said her father. 'I thought I told you to stop talking about her like that!'

'Is there another daughter at this house?' said the King's man, overhearing the conversation.

'No!' cried the stepmother.

'Yes!' cried the father in perfect unison[42]. 'She's right here.'

He left Greta and took Cinderella by her arm.

'Don't be afraid, dear.'

'No, that's not fair!' cried Greta.

'Everyone shall have a chance,' said the King's man. 'Those were the Prince's words. Now, my dear, here are the shoes.'

The man handed Cinderella the shoes with an expression of "let's get this over with[43]". Cinderella lowered her head and slipped them on.

They fit as perfectly as the night before, and immediately she felt the same magic flowing through her. She raised her head and smiled, walking forward with the grace of a swan and curtseying to the King's man.

'It's her! I didn't recognise you in the dirt and dust, and wearing such rags, but you are one and the same!'

'I may not be a foreign princess, but hopefully I am enough for the Prince.'

*A girl curtseying (pronunciation **KURT-see**)*

'More than enough!' cried the Prince, and jumped out of the carriage.

He had been hiding there the whole time, watching the scene!

'You are a most beautiful girl, and you have had to deal with such an ugly family.' He knelt down before her, taking her hand in his. 'I shall not ask your father for permission to marry you, because I wish it so strongly that no force on earth could stop me. Bridget, will you be mine?'

'Yes!' said the girl, and he pulled her into a kiss.

Despite her dirty appearance, despite the people watching, despite the crying of her sisters and stepmother, it was the most magical moment of her life. Everything else melted away, and all there was was her and the Prince.

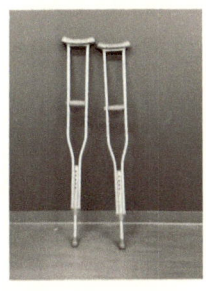

When you hurt your legs, you can use crutches to help you walk.

They had their wedding a few weeks later. Even though they had treated her like dirt, she made sure to invite her whole family. Her sisters came on crutches, unable to walk properly due to their mutilated[44] feet. Her stepmother refused to come.

Before the ceremony, her father took her aside to speak to her.

'I'm so sorry, Bridget. I was a terrible father. I pretended not to see, or I wished not to see, everything that was going on. I neglected you, and focussed on my work, and I let that awful woman ruin your life. When I see what she did to her own daughters...'

'What will you do, Father?'

'I am leaving her, and taking Freta and Greta with me.'

Cinderella's heart ached. For so many years she felt like she had lost her father, but now he was here again. She couldn't lose him again.

'Come live with us, in the castle.'

He laughed bitterly. 'I shouldn't think the Prince will want us here after he saw how awful we were. No, we will go and live a simple life, and I will teach those girls to be good and nice. You deserve your happiness, my dear.'

'But you'll come and visit, won't you?'

'Of course. I love you, Bridget. I'm just sorry I didn't show it properly.'

So Cinderella went and got married. But she was not Cinderella anymore, but Bridget, because she no longer had to stoop[45] in the fireplace and sweep up the ashes. She was going to be a queen, and she would never have to do such awful chores again, or put up with her horrible stepmother and stepsisters.

As the bride and groom kissed, a pair of birds flew happily around them, and far away, in the garden of a certain house, a hazel tree blew in the breeze.

AUTHOR'S NOTE

Thank you so much for reading *Easy Stories in English for Advanced Learners*! I hope you enjoyed the book and found it helpful.

If you did enjoy the book, please think about writing a review[1]. Reviews will help other people find the books, and the more people read the books, the more I will be able to write!

If you want language learning advice, you can join my email newsletter. Every two weeks I will send you an email telling you the best ways to study English. If you join now, you can get my free PDF 'My Top 10 Language Learning Advice'.

Go to EasyStoriesInEnglish.com/Email to join! Or you can scan the QR code below:

You can find over a hundred stories, including audio and transcripts, at EasyStoriesInEnglish.com. Scan the QR code below to go there:

Or you can find the podcast on Spotify or Apple Podcasts!

If you *really* enjoyed the book and have something to say, you can email me at Ariel@EasyStoriesInEnglish.com. I love hearing from my readers and listeners, so don't be shy!

Now that you've read the advanced level of this book, why not try a book for native speakers? Find a topic that interests you, and if it's too hard, choose another book until you find one that you can easily read. Take your English to the next level today!

VOCABULARY EXPLANATIONS AND REFERENCES

WHY YOU MUST READ

1. **To put it bluntly** = I will say it in a short, impolite way
2. 100 People, *100 People: A World Portrait* <https://www.100people.org/statistics-100-people/> [accessed 4 January 2021].
3. Stephen Krashen, *The Power of Reading - Stephen Krashen* (5 April 2012) <https://www.youtube.com/watch?v=DSW7gmvDLag> [accessed 4 January 2021].
4. **Proficiency** (pronunciation **pruh-FIH-shun-see**) = skill in a language
5. **To train your ear** = to get better at understanding fast speech
6. **Dry** = boring
7. **Unfiltered** = not changed, not made weaker
8. **Juvenile delinquent reform centres** are places (centres) to help young people (juveniles) change themselves and get better. These are young people who have committed crimes (delinquents). So basically, they are schools to help children who have had serious problems.
9. Stephen Krashen, *The Power of Reading - Stephen Krashen* (5 April 2012) <https://www.youtube.com/watch?v=DSW7gmvDLag> [accessed 4 January 2021].
10. **The Fiji islands** (pronunciation **FEE-jee EYE-lands**) = a country made of islands east of Australia
11. **Sustained silent reading** = reading in silence for a long time
12. Warwick B. Elley, 'The Potential of Book Floods for Raising Literacy Levels', *International Review Of Education*, 46, (2000), 233-255
13. **To replicate a study** = to do a study with the same conditions but in a different place to see if the results are the same
14. **To memorise** = to make yourself remember something
15. **A podcast** = a show that you can listen to on your phone, like a radio programme

16. **Fairy tales** = famous stories like Cinderella and Hansel and Gretel, which people usually tell to children
17. Stephen Krashen, 'Aesthetic Reading: Efficient Enough', *Journal Of English Language Teaching*, 62.2, (2020), 3-4.
18. Jeff McQuillan, 'Where Do We Get Our Academic Vocabulary? Comparing the Efficiency of Direct Instruction and Free Voluntary Reading', *The Reading Matrix*, 19.1, (2019), 129-138.
19. Heather Rolls, Michael P.H. Rogers, 'Science-specific technical vocabulary in science fiction-fantasy texts: A case for 'language through literature'', *English for Specific Purposes*, 48, (2017), 44-56.
20. **Time and time again** = many times, again and again
21. **To put a theory to the test** = to test a theory
22. **Duolingo** = a popular website for learning languages
23. **A transcript** = when you have a podcast or a radio show and you write down all the words as a text
24. **Latin American** = people from Latin America, countries like Peru, Argentina, Mexico and so on
25. **To converse** = to have a conversation, to chat
26. **To memorise** = to make yourself remember something
27. **To dive into books** = to spend lots of time with books, to get very interested in books
28. Stephen Krashen, 'Self-Selected Fiction: The Path to Academic Success?', *CATESOL Newsletter*, (2020), 1-2.
29. **Second language acquisition** = learning a second language, learning a language that isn't your first language (native language)
30. Stephen Krashen, 'The Case for Narrow Reading', *Language Magazine*, 3.5, (2004), 17-19.
31. Marcella Hu, Paul Nation, 'Unknown Vocabulary Density and Reading Comprehension', *Reading In A Foreign Language*, 13.1, (2000), 403-430
32. **Comprehensible** (pronunciation **kom-pruh-HEN-sih-bul**) = can be understood
33. **To butter something** = to put butter on something
34. **A caller** = someone who is calling you
35. Here is the text with no nonsense words:
    Jerry jumped out of bed and threw open the curtains. It was a beautiful day! He sang to himself as he went about his daily routine, pouring coffee and buttering toast. But then his phone rang, and the caller was so unexpected that he dropped his food on the floor.
36. The idea for this came from:

Marcos Benevides, *Extensive Reading: How easy is easy?* (2015) <https://www.slideshare.net/MarcosBenevides/how-easy-is-easy> [accessed 4 January 2021].

37. **Don't sweat it** = don't worry about it, relax
38. **A framework** = a structure, a system
39. **To reread** (pronunciation **REE-reed**) = to read something again
40. **To contradict something** = to go against something, to say something that is the opposite of something
41. **Audio** (pronunciation **AWW-dee-oh**) = sound

THE NORTH WIND AND THE SUN

1. **To bathe** (pronunciation **BAYTH**) = have a bath, swim
2. When you **crush** something, you squash it, make it completely flat. You usually crush things with your hand or your foot. For example, after you finish drinking a can of Coca Cola, you might crush it for fun. Or, if you are very cruel, you might enjoy crushing insects. When cooking, you often need to crush garlic with a knife.
3. **To slaughter** (pronunciation **SLAW-ter**) = to kill in a violent way
4. **BAM** is a sound you make when you hit something very hard.
5. **To hash out an argument** = to talk about something and try to come to an agreement over it
6. **Weakling** (pronunciation **WEEK-ling**) = a weak person
7. If you stop someone from getting air into their body, you **suffocate** them. You can suffocate someone by putting your hands around their neck, but this is not very nice!
8. **To scatter** = to separate quickly in many different directions
9. **A chill** = a coldness
10. When you **frown** (pronunciation **FRAUN**), you push your eyebrows together. When you are confused or angry, you frown. You shouldn't frown too much, though, because then you'll get wrinkles, lines on your forehead.
11. **Bathed the world in light** = Quickly covered the world with light
12. **To break a sweat** = to start sweating
13. When you loosely hang something over something else, you **sling** (past tense **slung**) it over it. For example, you might sling your coat over your arm, or sling a blanket over your bed.
14. **Exasperation** = annoyance, a state of being annoyed

STRANGE FRIENDS

1. **And indeed they were** = and, in fact, they were
2. An **altar** (pronunciation **AWL-tuh**) is a special table that you find in churches. It is at the front of the church.
3. '**Out of sight, out of mind**' is a phrase that means you quickly forget about things and people that you do not see. For example, if you are always eating chocolate and you want to stop, you can hide the chocolate. Because you don't see it, you'll think about it less—this is 'out of sight, out of mind'.
4. **To fantasise about** = to dream of, to think about something and wish you could have it
5. In Christianity, when a child is born, there is an event called a **christening** (pronunciation **KRIH-suh-ning**). You put water on the baby's head, and you give the baby a name. Two friends of the parents become the godmother and godfather. They say, 'I will help look after the child,' and they often give them presents and so on.
6. In Christianity, when a child is born, the parents choose a **godmother** and a **godfather**. They say, 'I will help look after the child,' and they often give them presents and so on. The godmother and godfather are chosen at an event called a christening.
7. **Crumbs** (pronunciation **KRUMZ**) = small pieces of bread, cake or biscuit
8. **To savour** (pronunciation **SAY-vuh**) = to enjoy food slowly, to enjoy it as much as possible
9. **Anticipation** = looking forward to something
10. **A smashing time** (British English) = an excellent time, a wonderful time
11. In Christianity, when a child is born, there is an event called a **christening** (pronunciation **KRIH-suh-ning**). You put water on the baby's head, and you give the baby a name. Two friends of the parents become the godmother and godfather. They say, 'I will help look after the child,' and they often give them presents and so on.
12. **A godchild** = the child who a godmother and godfather look after
13. **A housemate** = a person you live with, a person who shares your house
14. **Disposition** = personality, someone's qualities
15. **Pal** = friend

VOCABULARY EXPLANATIONS AND REFEREN... 125

16. **To muse to yourself** (pronunciation **MYOOZ**) = to think to yourself, to comment to yourself
17. **To grumble** = to complain quietly about something so that other people can't hear
18. **To fantasise about** = to dream of, to think about something and wish you could have it
19. **'Good things come in threes'** is a phrase. We say it when we have three good things together.
20. **A kitty** = a young cat, a baby cat
21. **To give pause** (pronunciation **PAWZ**) = to make you stop and think for a moment
22. **From top to bottom** = all over, the whole place
23. **To ponder** = to think very carefully about something
24. **To be deterred** = to be put off something, to be made less enthusiastic about doing something
25. **For all the good it will do you** = it won't do you any good, it will be pointless
26. **Gravely** = seriously
27. **To evoke memories** = to bring back memories, to remind you of old memories

THE VERY HUNGRY DRAGON

1. **Mid-morning snack** = a snack you have in the middle of the morning, usually 11am
2. **To nap** = to have a nap, to have a short sleep
3. **Dripping with fat** = there was so much fat on it that it was falling off in drops
4. **Hated jewels with a passion** (pronunciation **PAH-shun**) = hated jewels very much
5. When you **spit** (past tense **spat**), you throw water or food out of your mouth. In the UK, people don't spit outside, but in the past, people used to eat tobacco and spit it out. If you eat some very bad food, you might spit it out.
6. **Rubies** = a type of red jewel
7. **Emeralds** (pronunciation **EM-uh-ruld**) = a type of green jewel
8. **Amethysts** (pronunciation **AM-uh-thist**) = a type of purple jewel
9. **Vomit** = what you have when you throw up, when you are sick

10. **Creep** (past tense **crept**) means to go very slowly and quietly. When you creep, you don't hit your feet down loudly on the ground. Maybe you wake up in the middle of the night and want chocolate, but you don't want to wake up your family, so you creep to the kitchen.
11. **Stomach rumble** = a loud noise your stomach makes when you are hungry
12. **Bland** = has no flavour, tastes of nothing
13. **To munch** = to eat slowly and very loudly
14. **To crunch** = to chew very hard food so that it makes a loud noise
15. **Overjoyed** = very happy
16. A **merchant** is a person who sells things. In the past, merchants travelled to different countries and sold things there. Now, we have trucks and aeroplanes to carry things and sell them. A **merchant road** is a road that merchants travel on.
17. **Faraway** (pronunciation **far-uh-WAY**) = a place that is far away, not close
18. **Laden with** = heavy with, carrying lots of
19. **Caravan** = an old type of cart
20. When you eat a lot of food or drink a lot quickly, you might **burp**. You let out lots of air from your stomach very quickly, and it makes a loud noise. It is not polite to burp, so usually only children do it. Some food and drink can make you burp very easily. For example, Coca Cola can make you burp a lot.
21. **Had never seen the likes of before** = they had never seen anything like that before
22. **To hibernate** (pronunciation **HAI-buh-nayt**) = to sleep for a very long time, like a bear in winter
23. **Inconsiderate** (pronunciation **in-kun-SIH-der-ut**) = not thoughtful, not considering the feelings of other people
24. **Crawl** = to move on your hands and knees, like an insect
25. **Creep** (past tense **crept**) means to go very slowly and quietly. When you creep, you don't hit your feet down loudly on the ground. Maybe you wake up in the middle of the night and want chocolate, but you don't want to wake up your family, so you creep to the kitchen.
26. **To devour** (pronunciation **dih-VAU-uh**) = to eat very quickly when you are hungry
27. **Mid-morning snack** = a snack you have in the middle of the morning, usually 11am

DOGGO AND KITTY DO THEIR LAUNDRY

1. **To get on swimmingly with someone** = to get on very well
2. **To long** = to want very much
3. **Alas** (pronunciation **uh-LASS**) = unfortunately, oh no!
4. **It was not meant to be** = fate did not allow it, it could not happen
5. **To wriggle** = to move like a worm, to bend and turn quickly
6. **To loathe** = to hate very much
7. **Not a stitch of clothing to be found** = no clothes to be found, there wasn't a single piece of clothing
8. When you don't want someone to hear or see you, you **sneak** (past tense **snuck** or **sneaked**). For example, if you want to steal something from your brother's room, you might wait until he is sleeping and sneak inside. You walk very slowly and quietly, and you try to stay in the dark so that people don't see you. Thieves are usually very good at sneaking.
9. **To take on the air of** = to act like something, to pretend to be something
10. **To strain** = to struggle, to try very hard
11. **Lipstick** = makeup that you put on your lips, usually red
12. **To glitter** = to shine brightly like stars
13. **To heave** = to carry something very heavy
14. **Seeing as** = since, because
15. **Revolting** = absolutely disgusting
16. When you **spit** (past tense **spat**), you throw water or food out of your mouth. In the UK, people don't spit outside, but in the past, people used to eat tobacco and spit it out. If you eat some very bad food, you might spit it out.
17. **The very soap** = the same soap, that exact soap
18. **Glee** = childish happiness
19. **To scrub** = to rub strongly
20. **To ponder** = to think very carefully about something
21. **To leap** (pronunciation **LEEP**) = to jump very high
22. **To towel something off** = to dry something with a towel
23. **Dripping wet** = very wet, so wet that water is falling off
24. When you **turn your nose up** at something, you think it is horrible or disgusting. You feel **disgust**.

25. When you rub soap on your hands with water, it creates a thick white substance called **lather** (pronunciation **LAA-thuh**), which you use to clean your hands. You **lather up**.
26. **To clamber** = to climb with your hands and feet, to climb awkwardly
27. **In no time flat** = in no time, very quickly
28. **To poke your head out** = to put your head out, to move your head out
29. **Bone-tired** = very tired

DOGGO AND KITTY TEAR THEIR TROUSERS

1. **To get on swimmingly with someone** = to get on very well
2. **To ponder** = to think very carefully about something
3. **At any rate** = anyway
4. **Poked his nose through the window** = put his nose through the window, looked outside
5. **Parasol** (pronunciation **PAH-ruh-sol**) = an umbrella for the sun
6. **Cooped up** = stuck inside, unable to go outside
7. **To bite back** = to insult someone who has just insulted you
8. **Presentable** = looks nice enough to show to other people
9. **Hide-and-seek** is a game that children play. One child closes their eyes and counts: one, two, three, four… The other children run and hide somewhere. Then the first child has to find them.
10. **To gape** = to open your mouth very wide because you are surprised at something
11. **Spry** (pronunciation **SPRAI**) = fast, active, lively
12. When you have the same idea as a friend, you can say, '**Great minds think alike!**'. Basically, you are saying that you are both clever for having the same idea.
13. **To giggle** = to laugh nervously, to laugh like a girl
14. **A crying shame** = a big shame, a very sad situation
15. **Chin up** (British) = cheer up, don't feel so bad
16. **To bid farewell** = to say goodbye
17. **I spy something** (pronunciation **SPAI**) = I see something
18. **A booming voice** = a loud, deep voice
19. **To unravel** = to come apart, to break apart, to undo a knot

20. **To peck** = when a bird hits something with its mouth
21. **To wriggle** = to move like a worm, to bend and turn quickly
22. **A seamstress** (pronunciation **SEEM-struss**) = a woman who makes and repairs clothes
23. **To bid farewell** = to say goodbye
24. **Taken aback** = very surprised or shocked
25. When you want to give someone a suggestion for a plan, you say **'I'll tell you what'**.
26. **To squeak** = to make a very loud and high sound, like a mouse or an old tap
27. **To stand guard** = to stand by something and protect it, to wait for someone to come out
28. **...to boot** = as well as that, on top of that
29. **To giggle** = to laugh nervously, to laugh like a girl
30. **To stride** = to walk with big steps, to walk quickly
31. **Unorthodox** (pronunciation **un-AWW-thuh-doks**) = not following the usual rules, doing things in a strange way

DOGGO AND KITTY BAKE A CAKE

1. **To get on swimmingly with someone** = to get on very well
2. **Wondrous** = wonderful
3. **To ponder** = to think very carefully about something
4. **To adore** = to love very much
5. **Clean out of** = there were none, there was nothing
6. **To improvise** = to make it up as you go along
7. **Battered** = old and damaged
8. **A sandpit** = a box with lots of sand in it that children play in
9. **Wondrous** = wonderful
10. **To ooh and aah** = to say 'Ooh!' and 'Aah!', to be amazed by something
11. **Culinary** (pronunciation **KUH-lih-nair-ee**) = to do with food
12. **To ponder** = to think very carefully about something
13. **Divine** = very good
14. **Horrid** = horrible
15. **To adore** = to love very much
16. **To sniff** = to smell
17. **Horrid** = horrible

18. **Stomach rumble** = a loud noise your stomach makes when you are hungry
19. A **tail** is a long thing that animals have on their backs. Dogs, cats, foxes and so on all have tails. Humans do not have tails. When dogs are happy, they **wag** their tails, they move their tails quickly.
20. **An apron** (pronunciation **AY-prun**) is a piece of clothing you wear when you cook, so that you don't spill food on yourself.
21. **Batter** = a mixture of flour, eggs and milk that you use to make cakes
22. **Greasy** (pronunciation **GREE-see**) = has a lot of oil in it, has a lot of fat in it, like burgers, chips, bacon and so on
23. A **tail** is a long thing that animals have on their backs. Dogs, cats, foxes and so on all have tails. Humans do not have tails. When dogs are happy, they **wag** their tails, they move their tails quickly.
24. **Oh my goodness!** = a polite way of saying 'oh my God!'
25. **To heave** = to work with something very heavy
26. **To reduce something** (pronunciation **rih-DYOOS**) = to make something smaller
27. **To shove** (pronunciation **SHUV**) = to push
28. **A windowsill** = the shelf at the bottom of a window
29. **To skip** = to walk by jumping from one foot to the other, like a child
30. **To waft** (pronunciation **WOFT**) = (for a smell) to travel through the air
31. **Stomach rumble** = a loud noise your stomach makes when you are hungry
32. **To water** = to make water, to give out water
33. **Without a moment's hesitation** = without hesitating at all
34. **Horrified** = extremely shocked
35. 'Mt.' is short for 'mount', which we use when giving names of mountains. **Mt. Everest** is the tallest mountain in the world, and it is in the Himalayas. It is also known as Qomolangma.
36. **No offence** = something you say when you don't want to offend someone
37. **To budge** = to move slightly
38. **To whine** = to make a sound like a sad child, to complain

SLEEPING BEAUTY

1. **To mourn** = to cry for someone who has died
2. **Beloved** = loved
3. **Compassion** = love for others, caring about the suffering of others
4. **To dye** = to change the colour of something
5. A **compliment** is when you say something nice about someone else. For example, 'Oh, you look nice today!' or 'You're really good at cooking!'
6. **Gladiator** (pronunciation **GLAH-dee-ay-tuh**) = a man who fights other men in a stadium as a sport
7. **An omen** = a bad sign about the future, a message about the future
8. **A throne** = a big chair that the King sits on
9. **A chest** = a strong box made of wood used to store things
10. **Your Majesty** = a polite way to call the King or Queen
11. **A howling wind** = a very loud wind, a horrible wind
12. A **wrinkle** is a line in your face. People get wrinkles when they get old. People usually get wrinkles around their mouth, around their eyes and on their forehead.
13. **A raincloud personified** = a raincloud turned into a person, a human form of a raincloud
14. **Bony** = clearly showing the bone, thin and hard
15. A **(magic) spell** is a piece of magic. When you are **under a spell**, someone is using magic on you, and they can control you.
16. **Intricate** = complicated and beautiful
17. **In the pit of her stomach** = at the bottom of her stomach
18. **To glare** = to look with hatred in your eyes
19. **Wicked** = very evil
20. **Spell was broken** = the magic spell was broken, it finished
21. **Beloved** = loved
22. **Raindrops** = drops of rain
23. **Sought** (pronunciation **SAWT**) = past tense of **to seek**
24. **A healer** = a person who heals, a person who helps with health problems, usually using magic
25. **A magician** (pronunciation **muh-JIH-shun**) = someone who does magic
26. **A curse** = a type of bad magic that is very difficult to remove
27. **Fast asleep** = very deeply asleep
28. **A potion** = a magic drink

29. **Heartbroken** = has a broken heart, is very sad
30. **Slumber** = sleep
31. **In a vain attempt** = trying to do something but failing
32. **Watery** = made of water
33. **Seafoam** = the white stuff you find on the top of the water, especially when waves hit the beach
34. **To despise** = to hate strongly
35. **To tear apart** = to pull apart, to rip into pieces
36. **To crumble down** = to break into pieces and fall apart
37. **Every part** = in all ways
38. **Woke up with a start** = woke up suddenly and jumped
39. **Without hesitation** = without hesitating
40. **A throne** = a big chair that the King sits on
41. **Lustful** = thinking a lot about sex
42. **Dove** = past tense of **to dive** (also **dived**)
43. **To toss aside** = to throw aside easily
44. **Resignation** = accepting something awful that is going to happen, not fighting back
45. **To devour** = to eat quickly
46. **Ashes** are what you get when you burn something. When you burn something with fire, it goes black, and then it turns into thin grey things called ashes. When you burn wood, you get ashes. Also, when someone dies, you might have their body burnt, cremated, and then you can keep their ashes.
47. **To cleanse** (pronunciation **CLENZ**) = to clean, to make clean

ONE-EYED, TWO-EYED, THREE-EYED

1. **To despise** = to hate strongly
2. **A fringe** (British; pronunciation **FRINJ**) = hair that goes over your head, hair that goes over your eyes
3. **They got caught in the fringe** = they got stuck in the fringe, they bumped together
4. **A suitor** (pronunciation **SOO-tuh**) = a man who is looking for a wife
5. **I have searched far and wide** = I have searched everywhere
6. **Sought** (pronunciation **SAWT**) = past tense of **to seek**
7. **She's not my type** = she is not the type of woman that I like, she is not the right woman for me

VOCABULARY EXPLANATIONS AND REFEREN... 133

8. **A brat** = a horrible child who behaves badly
9. **A sob story** = a story to make someone feel sad about you, a story that makes someone feel sorry about you
10. **To shoot down an idea** = to tell someone that you think their idea is stupid without considering it properly
11. **To starve someone** = to give someone no food so they get thin or maybe die
12. **To overwork someone** = to make someone work too hard
13. **To toil away** = to work very hard, to work for a very long time
14. **Crumbs** = small pieces of bread, cake or biscuit
15. **Lazybones** = a lazy person
16. **Peckish** (British) = a bit hungry, quite hungry
17. **No offence** = something you say when you don't want to offend someone
18. After someone says 'no offence', if you were not actually offended, you can say '**none taken**', to mean 'I was not offended'.
19. **Wicked** = very evil, very bad
20. **Crumbs** = small pieces of bread, cake or biscuit
21. **To starve someone** = to give someone no food so they get thin or maybe die
22. **To morph** = to transform, to change
23. **Famished** (pronunciation **FAH-misht**) = very hungry
24. **To devour** (pronunciation **dih-VAU-uh**) = to eat very quickly when you are hungry
25. **To murmur** = to talk very quietly, to talk in an unclear way
26. When you **frown** (pronunciation **FRAUN**), you push your eyebrows together. When you are confused or angry, you frown. You shouldn't frown too much, though, because then you'll get wrinkles, lines on your forehead.
27. **To eat your fill** = to eat enough to fill you up
28. **To send someone into a frenzy** = to make someone go mad with anger
29. **They could not fathom** (pronunciation **FAH-thum**) = they could not understand
30. **A brat** = a horrible child who behaves badly
31. **To toil away** = to work very hard, to work for a very long time
32. **To scowl** (pronunciation **SKAUL**) = to make a sound like 'Ugh!' when you are annoyed
33. **A goatherd** (pronunciation **GOTE-herd**) = a person who looks after goats

34. **To weep** = to cry a lot
35. **To sleep soundly** = to sleep deeply
36. **To skip** = to walk by jumping from one foot to the other, like a child
37. **Bleary** = when your eyes look tired and your eyelids hang down
38. **To tag along with someone** = to join someone, to follow behind someone
39. **Work-shy** = doesn't like work, is lazy
40. **Smugly** = thinking she is better, feeling better than her
41. When you do a series of things in a specific order and way, that's a **ritual**. For example, your morning ritual might be to make coffee in a specific way and enjoy it while looking out of the window. Rituals are often an important part of religion. For example, marriage is an important ritual for many people, as you say things and do things in a very specific way.
42. **A goatherd** (pronunciation **GOTE-herd**) = a person who looks after goats
43. **To weep** = to cry a lot
44. **A fringe** (British; pronunciation **FRINJ**) = hair that goes over your head, hair that goes over your eyes
45. **A hearty** (pronunciation **HAR-tee**) **meal** = a filling and healthy meal
46. **To feverishly explain** = to explain in a very excited way
47. A **wrinkle** is a line in your face. People get wrinkles when they get old. People usually get wrinkles around their mouth, around their eyes and on their forehead.
48. A **witch** is an evil woman, a very bad woman, who does magic. Witches have black cats as pets, they wear big black hats and fly around. In *Harry Potter*, Hermione is a very successful witch. The musical *Wicked* is about witches.
49. **To eavesdrop** = to secretly listen to a conversation
50. **Strewn with tears** (pronunciation **STROON**) = covered with tears
51. **To make sure someone's sacrifice is not in vain** = to make sure someone did not sacrifice themselves for nothing, to make sure that the goat's death has meaning
52. **Raucous laughter** (pronunciation **RAW-cuss**) = loud, unpleasant laughter
53. **To resolve to do something** = to make a serious decision
54. **Distraught** (pronunciation **dis-TRAWT**) = very worried and upset
55. **Bony** = clearly showing the bone, thin and hard

56. **To taunt** (pronunciation **TAWNT**) = to make fun of someone, to laugh at someone
57. **To shy away from** = to move shyly away from something
58. **To marvel at something** = to look at something and think 'Wow!' because it is so amazing
59. **A stern look** = a strict look, a severe look
60. A **witch** is an evil woman, a very bad woman, who does magic. Witches have black cats as pets, they wear big black hats and fly around. In *Harry Potter*, Hermione is a very successful witch. The musical *Wicked* is about witches.
61. **To pluck** = to quickly pull something away from something else, for example flowers, plucking a hair out, plucking a feather out of a bird and so on
62. **To be mesmerised** = to have your attention completely taken by something, to be amazed by something
63. **To have your sights set on something** = to be very focussed on something, to be very interested in something
64. **To despise** = to hate strongly
65. **To glitter** = to shine brightly like stars
66. **To badger someone about something** = to annoy someone about something, to keep asking someone about something
67. **Uncooperative** = not cooperative, not willing to work together with someone
68. **Fakely** = in a non-sincere way, in a way that shows that she didn't really find it funny
69. **Flexible** = able to bend easily
70. **Idle** (pronunciation **EYE-dul**) = lazy
71. **Her throw was true** = she threw accurately, her throw worked
72. **To dust something off** = to wipe dust or dirt off something
73. **I haven't the foggiest!** = I have no idea, I do not know at all
74. **Profusely** (pronunciation **pro-FYOOS-lee**) = to do something a lot, more than normal
75. **To have a meltdown** = to get so emotional that you collapse, to lose all control of yourself
76. **To yank out** = to pull out strongly
77. **To glisten** = to shine like sunlight on the ocean
78. **Overcome with emotion** = she had so many emotions that she didn't know what to do, she had so many feelings she couldn't do anything

THE BOY WHO KNEW NO FEAR

1. **To loathe** (pronunciation **LOTHE**) = to hate and be disgusted by something
2. **Idle** (pronunciation **EYE-dul**) = lazy
3. **A good-for-nothing** = a person who can do nothing well
4. When you **shudder**, you shake. You move a bit because you are scared or cold. The hairs on your arms stand up. If you don't want to show that you are scared, you can try and stop yourself from shuddering. But sometimes you are so scared that you cannot stop yourself.
5. **Woodwork** (British) = learning to make things from wood
6. **To smirk** = to smile in a very satisfied and confident way
7. **To eavesdrop** = to secretly listen to a conversation
8. **At length** = in great detail, for a long time
9. **To light up** = to suddenly become very excited and happy
10. **The Lord** = God
11. When you don't want someone to hear or see you, you **sneak** (past tense **snuck** or **sneaked**). For example, if you want to steal something from your brother's room, you might wait until he is sleeping and sneak inside. You walk very slowly and quietly, and you try to stay in the dark so that people don't see you. Thieves are usually very good at sneaking.
12. **Bedsheets** = the sheets you use in your bed
13. **Weary** (pronunciation **WEE-rih-lee**) = very tired
14. **To be up to something** = to be doing something wrong or secret, to be doing something
15. **That'll teach you** = that will show you, you won't do that again
16. **To pester** = to bother, to annoy
17. **Horrified** = very scared or shocked
18. **To whimper** = to make a sound like a sad dog because you are scared or in pain
19. **A pervert** = a very strange person, a person with strange sexual behaviour
20. **To shrug** = to raise your shoulders when you are doubtful, do not know something, or do not care about something
21. **To loathe** (pronunciation **LOTHE**) = to hate and be disgusted by something

22. A **conman** is a man who tries to **con** people. When you con someone, you try to trick them and take their money. For example, someone might talk to you in the street and say, 'I see that you're bald. I have a magic drink here. If you drink it, you will grow hair. You just have to pay me £1000.' But actually, the drink doesn't do anything, and if you buy it, the conman has conned you.
23. **Smugly** = thinking he is better, feeling better than other people
24. When you are doing something because you are kind and generous, and not because you want something in return, you can say that you are doing it **out of the goodness of your heart**. Often, people use this sarcastically. That is, they do not really mean it.
25. A **guarantee** (pronunciation **GAH-run-tee**) is a formal piece of writing that says that certain promises will be met. For example, when you buy a car you might get a guarantee that it will not break in the first year. Guarantee can also mean 'to assure' or 'to make sure', so people often say, 'I guarantee you this will happen,' for example.
26. A **cloak** (pronunciation **CLOKE**) = a big piece of clothing like a coat
27. A **figure of speech** is when you say something that has two meanings. There is a literal meaning, the direct meaning of the words, but you do not mean this. You mean a metaphorical meaning, a message that the other person has to understand. For example, when you say, 'He has a heart of stone,' you are not literally saying that his heart is made of stone. You are saying that he is unkind and cold. That is the metaphor.
28. **As the night drew in** = as the night arrived, as the night came in
29. **To sway** = to move left and right, to move from side to side
30. **Oblivious** (pronunciation **uh-BLIH-vee-us**) = unaware of what is happening around you, not knowing what is happening around you
31. **To set something on fire** = to make something start burning, to put fire on something
32. **No teacher worth their salt** = no real teacher, no proper teacher, no good teacher
33. **Huffy** = complaining a lot, annoyed at being made to do something boring
34. **Leaping to his feet** (pronunciation **LEE-ping**) = jumping to his feet, jumping and standing up
35. **Dismayed** = feeling very worried and surprised

36. When you **frown** (pronunciation **FRAUN**), you push your eyebrows together. When you are confused or angry, you frown. You shouldn't frown too much, though, because then you'll get wrinkles, lines on your forehead.
37. **Compensation** = a reward for doing something, something to make up for something bad you had to do
38. **To inhabit a place** = to live in a place
39. **To get someone's hand in marriage** = to be allowed to marry someone
40. A **jackpot** is the best prize you can win in a game. Usually, it is used in gambling, which is when people play with money and can win more money if they are lucky. If you get the jackpot, you will be very lucky. Generally, when you win something great, you can say, 'Jackpot!'
41. A **lathe** (pronunciation **LAYTH**) is a thing that turns something around. So when you make pottery, you use a lathe. Pottery is mugs, pots and so on. You put the clay, the thing you use to make pottery, on the lathe, and it turns it around. Then you use your hands to make the pottery. You can also use lathes to make things out of wood, for example.
42. **Woodwork** (British) = learning to make things from wood
43. **To shrug** = to raise your shoulders when you are doubtful, do not know something, or do not care about something
44. **Mind your business** = that's none of your business, stop asking questions that you don't need to know the answers to
45. **To snatch something away** = to pull away very quickly, to take something in a rude way
46. **To cast a magic spell** = to use magic
47. **To swarm** = to move in a large group, like bees or flies
48. A **beast** (pronunciation **BEEST**) = a horrible animal
49. **At the stroke of midnight** = as soon as midnight came
50. **Crawl** means to move forward by lying down and using your hands and feet. People only crawl when they are trying to stay hidden, for example soldiers who are trying to secretly get into a building. Snakes and insects always crawl, because they cannot stand up.
51. **To lull someone to sleep** = to put someone to sleep with calm, slow movements or a song
52. **To flip over** = to turn over
53. **The torso** = the human body without the head, neck, arms or legs

54. When you sew, there are various kinds of **stitches** you can make. They are ways of joining the thread. So **to stitch** is another word for 'to sew'. When you **stitch something back together**, you take something that is in pieces, torn apart, and sew it back together.
55. **To growl** = to make a low sound from the throat, like an angry dog
56. When you **roll your eyes**, you move your eyes around in a circle. You roll your eyes when someone does something stupid or strange, but you don't want to tell them directly.
57. **Oblivious** (pronunciation **uh-BLIH-vee-us**) = unaware of what is happening around you, not knowing what is happening around you
58. **At the stroke of midnight** = as soon as midnight came
59. **A coffin** = a box you go in when you die
60. **To devour** (pronunciation **dih-VAU-uh**) = to eat very quickly when you are hungry
61. When you **roll your eyes**, you move your eyes around in a circle. You roll your eyes when someone does something stupid or strange, but you don't want to tell them directly.
62. **A round of bowling** = a game of bowling
63. **To leer** = to stare in an unpleasant way
64. When you **strangle** someone, you put your hands around their neck and press down so that they stop getting air, so that they suffocate. If you strangle someone for a long time, they will die.
65. **To wield** (pronunciation **WEE-uld**) = to hold and use a weapon or a tool, such as an axe, a gun or a hammer
66. **To dangle** = to hang down and move left and right
67. **To beat someone until they're black and blue** = to beat someone until they have bruises, to beat someone until their skin is black and blue
68. **A chest** = a strong box made of wood used to store things
69. **A bearded man** = a man who has a beard
70. **To gasp** = to take a big breath because you are very surprised
71. **Hooray** = a word you say when you are very happy for someone

CINDERELLA

1. **Ashes** are what you get when you burn something. When you set something on fire, it burns, goes black and eventually turns into thin grey things called ashes, which float through the air. Wood

produces the most ashes, and if you have a traditional fireplace, you have to clean the ashes out regularly. Many people, when they die, choose to be cremated, burnt, and then their family keeps their ashes in a jar called an urn.
2. **A ball** = a big party with lots of dancing
3. **To gasp** = to take a big breath because you are very surprised
4. **To tailor** = to change clothes to fit someone
5. **To fashion** = to make into a particular shape
6. **It's not worthy of even a walk down the road** (pronunciation **WER-thee**) = it's not even good enough for a walk down the road
7. When you **embarrass** someone, you make them feel stupid. For example, if you are with your group of friends, and one of your friends is very short, and you say, 'Hey, shortie! Don't you want to be taller?' they might go red because they're embarrassed. In this case, if other people saw Cinderella, her family would be embarrassed, because she looks so bad.
8. **Holding back tears** = trying very hard to hide her tears
9. A **carriage** (pronunciation **KAH-rij**) is a vehicle, a way of getting around, like a car. Usually, carriages are pulled by horses, and someone sits on top of the carriage and tells the horses to move. Before cars existed, carriages were the main way of travelling.
10. **A gown** (pronunciation **GAUN**) = a dress
11. **Yet another nut fell** = one more nut fell
12. When you **pinch** someone, you pull together some of their skin between your fingers. It hurts quite a bit. When something really amazing happens to you, you might say, '**Pinch me, I'm dreaming**!' because you think that it must be a dream, and that if someone pinches you, you will wake up. So when Cinderella pinches herself, she is making sure that this is real and not a dream.
13. **The clock strikes eleven** = it is eleven o'clock and the clock makes a loud sound (DONG DONG) eleven times
14. **To put two and two together** means to figure out something obvious from the available information. Everyone knows that, if you add two and two, you get four. So if you see mud on the floor, and your dog is hiding in the bathroom and has muddy feet, you can put two and two together and figure out that it was your dog who brought the mud in.
15. **Something was up** = something was wrong, something was going on
16. **Vigour** (pronunciation **VIH-guh**) = energy

17. **To overhear** = to accidentally hear something, to hear a conversation that you're not a part of
18. **To dump** = to drop something in a rude way
19. **Lazybones** = a lazy person
20. When you **frown**, you push your eyebrows together. When you are confused or angry, you frown. You shouldn't frown too much, though, because then you'll get wrinkles, lines on your forehead.
21. **To gasp** = to take a big breath because you are very surprised
22. **To attend to a matter** = to deal with a problem
23. **Sternly** = strictly, severely
24. **To arch an eyebrow** = to raise an eyebrow
25. **I could have sworn** = I was absolutely sure
26. **Rags** = dirty old clothes
27. **To overhear** = to accidentally hear something, to hear a conversation that you're not a part of
28. **To burden someone** = to give someone a difficult task, to give someone something to worry about
29. **To outdo yourself** = to do something better than you ever have before
30. **Before the spell was broken** = before the magic ended
31. **To disintegrate** (pronunciation **dis-IN-tuh-grayt**) = to break into many small parts, to fall apart
32. **Her hair lost its bounce** = her hair stopped bouncing, her hair became flat
33. **To pull yourself together** = to regain control of your emotions, to handle your feelings
34. When you **seduce** (pronunciation **sih-DYOOS**) someone, you flirt with them, you say nice things to them, until they want to get into bed with you. In the past, it was common for men to seduce women. Sometimes, women would seduce men so that they would marry them.
35. **A grave expression** = a very serious expression
36. **To wait on someone hand and foot** = to serve someone's every need, to act like a servant for someone, to do everything for someone
37. When you want to give someone a suggestion for a plan, you say **'I'll tell you what'**.
38. **Snotarella** is a nickname that Greta has thought of for Cinderella. **Snot** is the dirty stuff you get in your nose. When you sneeze, snot comes out.

39. **To whine** = to make a sound like a sad child, to complain
40. **To stomp** = to walk with very heavy steps, to walk loudly
41. **What's all this racket about?** = what's all this noise for?
42. **To speak in unison** (pronunciation **YOO-nih-sun**) = to speak at the same time as someone else
43. **To get something over with** = to finish an unpleasant task
44. **Mutilated** = horribly damaged, extremely wounded
45. **To stoop** = to bend down in an uncomfortable way

AUTHOR'S NOTE

1. **A review** is when you write about a book you read, saying what you liked and didn't like, and give it a rating (1-5 stars).

IMAGE ATTRIBUTIONS

THE NORTH WIND AND THE SUN

'Cold?' by Antoine K is licensed under CC BY-SA 2.0.

THE VERY HUNGRY DRAGON

Dragon by Freepik is from Flaticon.com.
 'One whole, deli dill pickle' by National Cancer Institute is in the public domain.

DOGGO AND KITTY DO THEIR LAUNDRY

Paw by Freepik is from Flaticon.com; cropped.
 'The Religious Kibbutz Movement, Settlements in Israel' by The religious kibbutz archive is in the public domain.

'Diet Coke Mentos' by Michael Murphy is licensed under CC BY-SA 3.0.

'View from the Backenswarft on Hallig Hooge' by Michael Gäbler is licensed under CC BY 3.0.

DOGGO AND KITTY TEAR THEIR TROUSERS

'Greyhound with a brindle pattern' by L. Bower is in the public domain.

'Rose Prickles' by JJ Harrison is licensed under CC BY-SA 3.0.

'A needle and red string' by www.photos-public-domain.com is in the public domain.

Spiral by Smashicons is from Flaticon.com.

'Dvojitý rybářský uzel 2, Techmania, Plzeň' by Zpevdeste is licensed under CC BY-SA 4.0.

DOGGO AND KITTY BAKE A CAKE

'Springform Pan with the walls loosened from the finished product.' by RibbonsOfIndecision is licensed under CC BY-SA 3.0.

SLEEPING BEAUTY

Fairy by Flat Icons is from Flaticon.com.

'Cloak' by David Ring is in the public domain.

Wine Glass With Crack by Freepik is from Flaticon.com.

ONE-EYED, TWO-EYED, THREE-EYED

'One whole, deli dill pickle' by National Cancer Institute is in the public domain.

'Amneville Bison 27082010 4' by Vassil is in the public domain.

'Male impala profile' by Muhammad Mahdi Karim is licensed under the GNU Free Documentation License 1.2.

THE BOY WHO KNEW NO FEAR

Rope by Freepik is from Flaticon.com.

Axe by Freepik is from Flaticon.com.

Spiral by Smashicons is from Flaticon.com.

Paw by Freepik is from Flaticon.com; cropped.

Bowling by Freepik is from Flaticon.com.

Skull by Freepik is from Flaticon.com.

CINDERELLA

'Hazelnuts' by Fir0002 is licensed under CC BY-SA 3.0.

Bow by Freepik is from Flaticon.com.

'Lens culinaris seeds' by Rainer Zenz is in the public domain.

'MarmiForoTraianoRoma' by MM is in the public domain.

'AdhesivesForHouseUse004' by Babi Hijau is in the public domain.

'Curtsy (PSF)' by Pearson Scott Foreman is in the public domain.

'Axillary Crutches' by Jessica Fisher is licensed under CC BY-SA 4.0.

www.ingramcontent.com/pod-product-compliance
Lightning Source LLC
Chambersburg PA
CBHW021439080526
44588CB00009B/599